Drawings by Geoff Wood

Pen and ink illustrations by Sarah Halstead

Photography by Stephen Parnell

Other main source of illustrations: Rochdale Local Studies Library

TOAD LANE TO 'THE HEIGHTS'

and

THE BAUM RABBIT TALE

by
Marcia Bartlett

Map of Rochdale area showing locations including:

- Shaw Clough
- Cronkenshaw T.P.
- Carr Hill
- Hollows
- Heights
- Top of the Heights
- One Ash
- Rose Hill
- Field House Mill
- Ebors Nook
- The Town
- Boundary
- Lark Hill
- CRONKEYSHAW
- Green Bank Mill
- Fox Ho
- Don Inn House
- Falinge Fold
- Bent Meadows
- Field Head
- Jep Hous
- Green Hill
- Drown Hill
- Casson Gate
- Industry House
- Green Heyes Mill
- Mount Falinge
- Mean Wood
- Quarry Hill
- Spotland Bridge
- Charles Lane
- College Houses
- St James Church
- Spotland Workhouse
- Vale
- Holmes Mill
- Mitchel Hey
- Mount Front
- The Orchard
- Ellis Street

PREFACE

This book takes a look at life broadly along the route of
the old Rochdale and Burnley Turnpike Trust Road, from the
bottom of Toad Lane to the top of Heights Lane — with a few
diversions along the way.

I hope it will be of general interest to Rochdale people and to
visitors to the town, but its primary purpose is educational. It has
been written and illustrated for young people following Local
Studies Courses. The subject matter has been indexed to the
Sources of Reference to provide an easy starting point for the
individual or group research projects which may be stimulated by
the text.

I also hope schools will explore the dramatic opportunities the
book presents, for narration and improvisation, with projection of
visual material. A tape recording of the text made by Bernard
Cullen, graphic designer and amateur actor, is available to schools
through the Education Service.

It is written in my own adaptation of Blank Verse which combines
modern prose features with the traditional form; and is best read
aloud — with a touch of 'Lancashire' intonation!

The poetry is in the history
and history the stuff of poetry.

Marcia Bartlett
1989

Map c.1860
Thos. L. Whitehead, Surveyor, Rochdale.

Toad Lane ...

Toad Lane? Rochdalians will know the name,
and even folk who live elsewhere have heard
it's where the Rochdale Pioneers set up
their Co-op shop in eighteen forty four.

And now there's a museum there where you
can feel authentic atmosphere, and on
the wall outside, advertisements that take
you back into another time ... when Steam
Tramways Company published 'thrupny' fares;
and Mafeking's Relief was celebrated
by a brass band march all round the town;
and Circus came to Newgate, Christmas time,
December eighth - the year nineteen-o-one.

Next door is Mrs. Norbury's Toy Bazaar
and hospital for dolls; and next to that
a wine bar and a restaurant with gourmet
French cuisine, which carries on the name
'The Baum' - but though these are 'in character',
they're really not what old Toad Lane's about ...

So let's explore some aspects of its past.

First, how did Toad Lane get its name, d'you think?
It sounds odd now when so much part of town,
but in the sixteen hundreds and before,
its rural character was well-defined.

Undoubtedly, it's old: some say 'Th'owd Lane'
was once its name, and others say that 'toad'
refers to 'tod', a measurement for wool,
and, yet again, the German word for death
is thought appropriate because of tales
this poem will tell ... but in another poem
by William Nuttall published eighteen ten,
these lines appear - to set the record straight?

"And even here the croaking toad was seen,
To lurk i'th grass, and skim o'er Lord's-burne stream."

Perhaps there is no mystery at all?
The 'toad' in Toad Lane means quite simply TOAD?
But more about this question later on!

As well as toads, both sticklebacks and loaches
could be seen so clearly in the clean
pure water which arose from springs on lands
around Heights Lane, and wound through meadows where
Mount Pleasant and then Cheetham Street were built.

The stream's been channelled underground so can't
be seen today, but also wandered through
the meadowland which later came to be
St. Mary's graveyard in The Baum - then ran
into the River Roch in town, just by
'The Orchard', or Memorial Gardens now.

In seventeen forty five when Scottish troops
belonging to the Stuart rebel force
marched down Blackwater Street and then closed in
around the 'Union Hotel', where townsmen
(Messrs. Chadwick, Royds and Entwistle)
were grappling with inadequate defence,
this little Lordburn stream provided an
escape route for a few who dared not face
the kilted Lochiel of Glengarry and
'the foe', who - contrary to all reports
of most appalling crimes - seemed very well
behaved; and asked for lodgings for one night.

The only injuries for Toad Lane's
Doctor Moult to treat were somewhat trivial.
A Scotsman burnt by scalding dripping when
a cook called Betty found him over-friendly,
though her aftercare led to betrothal
and renouncement of Prince Charlie's cause.
And sword cuts on the face and arms of one
Rochdalian who tempted fate by driving
nails into the toe-caps of his clogs,
and picked an argument he couldn't win.

The full account of these events is worth
a read: Prince Charles' attempt to beat King George
was routed and he fled to France; the one
man from this town who joined his army (name
of Holt) was executed on the scaffold
in October seventeen forty six.

'The Union Hotel' was opposite the market end of The Walk.
Reproduced from the 1851 Ordnance Survey Map

❧ There's more to old Toad Lane than meets the eye.
In olden times it was a packhorse route,
which turned off up through Casson Gate to Syke,
and 'Galloways' (those ponies of a sturdy
Scottish breed) once carried lime to town.
But let's keep first to eighteenth century times,
and think about the way the lane was then.

In seventeen fifty five Toad Lane became
a Turnpike Road. Top end, near Falinge grounds
upon the left and Cronkeyshaw to right,
was later to be called Heights Lane (but this
took place a century ahead). It led
to Healey, Whitworth, Bacup and beyond -
the designated tollgate route to Burnley.

In seventeen ninety Falinge Road was made
and Whitworth Road in eighteen thirty six.

To show you what the lane was like, there's still
a narrow unmade track which winds from top
of Heights Lane round to Rudman Street and on
to Shawclough Road. 'Alicia Cottage' was
there then as three small cottages - made into
one about two hundred years ago.

'Alicia Cottage' at the top of Heights Lane and the old Turnpike Road leading down to Shawclough. See Map p76.

The Toad Lane pikeman (or the 'barrkeeper' so called) would stop all those who hadn't risked a fine by taking Foxholes Lane, and ask the sum of 'one and four', or two shillings per cart. One kindly pikeman was dismissed in seventeen seventy eight for only charging fourpence. Prior to that, in seventeen sixty nine, a man was gainfully employed in watching those who let their horses loose to cheat the pikeman at the Toad Lane bar.

'Brown Hill' c.1630s – 1950
See Map p4.

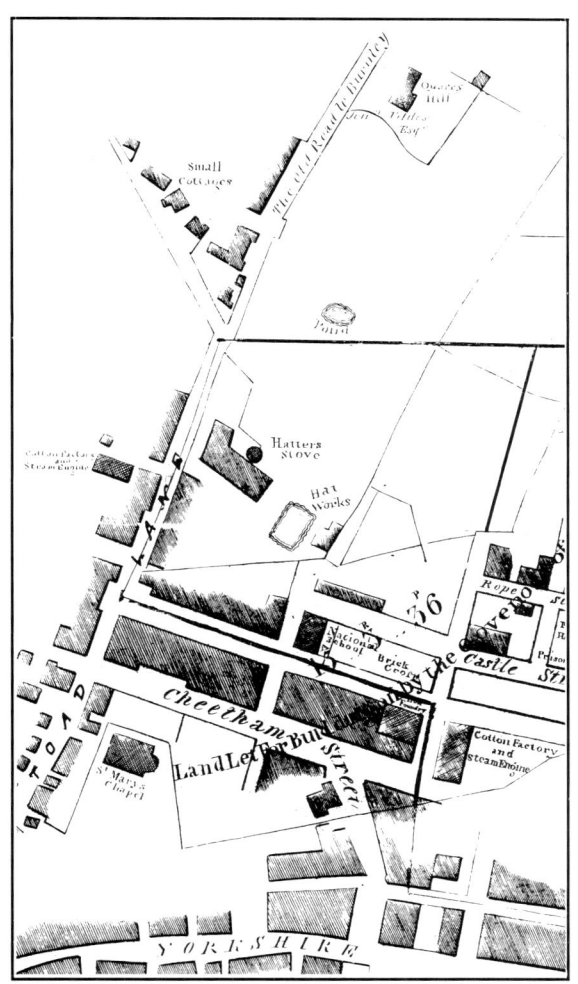

Reproduced from Waterworks Map 1816 by John Moorhouse, Manchester.

The system was corrupt, with tolls being leased
at auction and prices 'ringed' to keep them low.
But sometime after seventeen ninety one
when Falinge Road became the easier route,
the Toad Lane bar was closed, replaced by the
Swinerootings toll quite near 'The Healey' inn.

Where was the tollgate on Toad Lane? Between
'Brown Hill', the residence of Reverend Holme,
and Dyehouse owned by Thomas Fildes & Son -
on this old map it's shown as 'Hatter's Stove'.
But more exact than that it's hard to be.
The Reverend Edmund Holme was one of the
Trustees; and his son Thomas paid the sum
of four pounds and four shillings once a year
for carriages and horses to pass through.

Both gentlemen were buried in the garden
of 'Brown Hill', but later moved to more
appropriate rest at Parish Church when James Royds
bought the house in seventeen ninety four.
Of course this was a most irregular
affair, with Doctor Wray, the Vicar, not
consenting to present a sermon at
the funeral of the Reverend Edmund Holme,
whose aim had been to stop his sons from
selling off 'Brown Hill' as soon as he was dead.

Of all the folk who've had connections with
Toad Lane since it was just a winding track,
it's hard to try imagining how many
pairs of feet have trodden the same ground.

The names of ordinary folk are not
recorded well in any age, but it
would not be right to talk about this lane
without including families whose lives
were interlinked with both the lane and church,
and made their marks in different ways upon
the town ... so, something of the Brierleys from
the bottom of Toad Lane, but first a bit
about the Royds who started from the top.

They came from Yorkshire, sixteen forty one,
when there were just ten thousand people here.
As Wardle farmer-weavers first, they dealt
in wool, then grew to be a large and
influential family who purchased Falinge
lands and property, and registered
their pedigree to claim a family crest.

The houses most connected with their names
(at least around the top of old Toad Lane) -
'Mount Falinge', 'Brown Hill' and 'Green Hill': as to
the first, a poor facade remains within
the splendid grounds of Falinge Public Park.
There's something still about the place which makes
you think of carriages and crinolines
and croquet on the lawns ... a life apart
from weavers' up and down this ancient lane.
John Royds lived there (died seventeen ninety nine)
and then his son called James, who fathered nine.

The Royds' Coat of Arms

*Right: 'Mount Falinge'
See Map p4.*

❧ The famous Clement Royds was one of these.
He lived there too - died eighteen fifty four.
A most ambitious man who exercised
his Tory power in politics and other
roles as well. He owned a cotton mill,
a bank, was Magistrate, High Sheriff too,
and as a public figure was respected ...
and despised: in eighteen thirty eight
the Chartists' protest at the Poor Law named
the Magistrates to be 'removed', with
torchlight meetings held to urge the use of arms.

Three highwaymen robbed two of Clement's sons
in eighteen thirty five. But what of Royds'
connection with St. Mary's Church? He was
a Warden there and brother Edward was
Incumbent in the year eighteen nineteen.

A later Reverend, Joseph William Inchbald,
married Clement's sister Lucy when
he wed a second time ... so very many
Royds, and several Clements too, as time
went on ... It's not that easy to keep track,
but there's a plaque in St. Chad's Church that lists
the Royds who worshipped there. And now there are
some Rochdale streets that bear their names, as well
as Spotland churches from Royds' patronage -
St. Clement's, and St. Edmund's near the park.

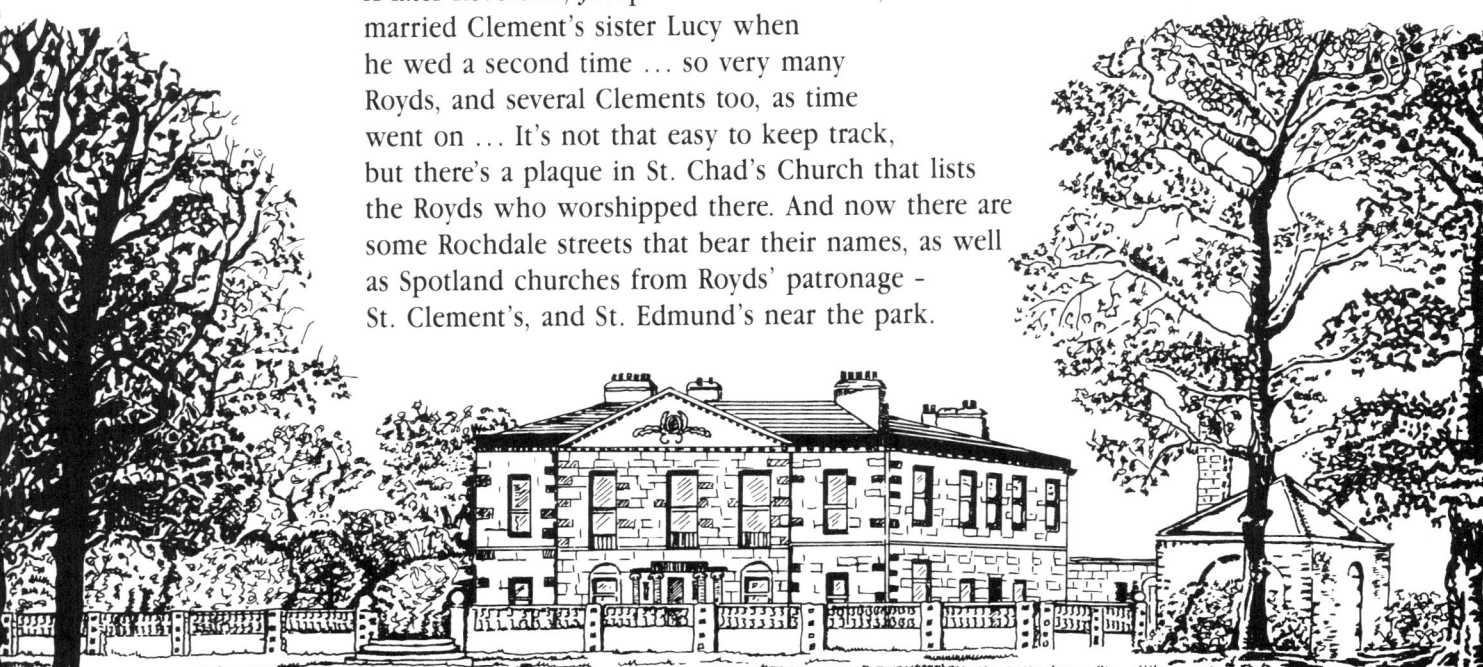

St. Mary's dates from seventeen forty two.
The situation at the time was that
the population of the town had been
increased "by reason of ye woollen
manufactures" and St. Chad's was over-full.

Of five outlying chapels, Ashworth,
Littleborough and Milnrow were the closest to
the town, so Rochdale centre's second church
was built twixt Toad Lane and the Lordburn stream.
The cost was just one thousand pounds, exactly
half of which was given by Samuel Chetham
(Castleton), the rest by small subscription.

It should be said before it seems that the
'Baum Chapel' was the only one to serve
this area's needs, St. Mary's is a Church
of England church, and there were several
Nonconformist chapels round Toad Lane, as well
as Toad Lane Wesleyan Chapel mentioned
later on. The Rochdale Congregationalists
had met from sixteen seventy two at least.

The Chapel in Blackwater Street for
Unitarians was built seventeen seventeen
and rebuilt eighteen fifty six; then there
were 'Providence' and 'Milton' not far off.
In recent times the Unitarians
have had to build again in Clover Street.
The new Salvation Army Hostel keeps
the name of 'Providence' alive today.

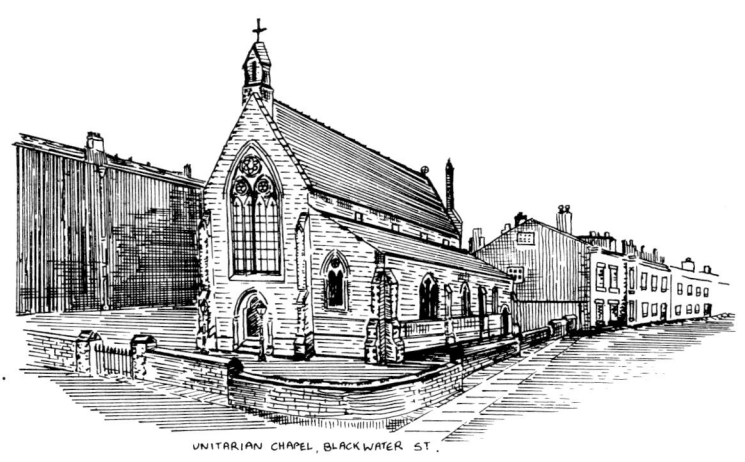

UNITARIAN CHAPEL, BLACKWATER ST.

John Ashworth's Chapel for the Destitute
on Baillie Street, from eighteen fifty eight,
was open for the poor of any creed,
or those of none at all, and filled a social
need in finding lodgings for the vagrants
of the streets and money for the sick.

The strength of Rochdale's Nonconformist faith
was evidenced in eighteen fifty one.
The Census of Religious Worship shows
a plethora of Chapels round about,
(and there were Meetings of the Quakers too),
whose worshippers exceeded those of the
Established Church. It was, of course, from this
strong base that Rochdale's 'Liberalism' sprang,
which came to have such influence in the town.

So, bearing this in mind, let's carry on!

At town end of Toad Lane the Brierleys lived
throughout the eighteenth century at least;
although this sometimes was spelt 'Brearley'.

When Benjamin was born in seventeen forty
one, St. Mary's Church was being built.
Well-known as 'Ben o'th' Coach', it's thought he was
an ostler at the 'Coach and Horses' inn
(pulled down in nineteen seventy four); in time
he married Alice Shore; and their son Joseph
married Ann, whose father Abraham Stott
(another Toad Lane man) exported rugs
throughout the world. Five sons survived the trials
of infancy: of these, another Benjamin
became a plumber in St. Mary's Place,
and Samuel fathered Henry who
became a lawyer in the town and wrote
his 'Reminiscences'; as to the rest -
the brothers James and John and Abraham ...

The youngster Henry Brierley was taken
by his father to St. Mary's Church
until the year of eighteen fifty three
or four and then went to St. Chad's. In fact
the Reverend William Inchbald christened him
in eighteen forty seven. And he recalls
his father taking out the eastern seats
from their own pew and bringing in a rustic
garden seat, so all the family
could face towards the East; before this act
the pew had always seated ten all round.
Such was his father's sense of ritual!

This same man, Samuel Brierley, wrote about
the Scottish rebels coming into town.
And his son Henry's better known as
Doctor Henry Brierley, public figure, now.

Doctor Henry Brierley

A Robert Schofield, Parish Clerk, who served
in both the Reverend Inchbald's and the Reverend
Cleare's incumbencies, and was the last
man to be buried at St. Mary's Church
in eighteen fifty five when Rochdale
20 Cemetery was made, was prone to using the
odd 'H', and words, a little out of place.
One Sunday when a dog strayed into church,
he cried in startling monologue: "Hextinguish
that dog!" - a word he'd heard applied to
putting out the candles. Another day
he called upon the homes of those who rented
pews to let them know a service would
be cancelled "in consequence of the Heclipse!"

The Clerk sat in the lowest of the three-tiered
pulpit seats, resplendent in red wig.
One deck of three remains to make the single
pulpit in St. Mary's Church today.

*St. Mary's Church, Wardleworth,
built 1742, known as 'The Baum Chapel'.*

St. Mary's Church rebuilt 1909-11.

But it was Henry's Uncle Abraham,
(who kept the books at Pilling's Mill and then
was married to James Pilling's daughter Anne,
and later owned a mill himself on Holland
Street) and his son James - their wives as well,
whose long association is well-marked
by gifts, including the baptismal font
in sculptured stone, with Sacrificial Lamb
and Ark and Dove and Fishes Three inlaid;
and several stained glass windows too from
eighteen sixty five to eighteen seventy four.

St. Mary's Vicar at the time was
Reverend Napier Sharpe, the church's first
true Vicar (prior to him all others being
Curates or Incumbents governed by
St. Chad's). He set the tone for much that still
holds true today of reverent and stately
worship practised at this church, and is
remembered too for innovations made
inside - the renovated chancel, and
the three-light crucifixion windows, which
divided now, are set inside the Jesus
Chapel and the Chapel of St. James.

The cross and candlesticks now resting on
the altar of St. James were stolen by
the 'Nonconformists', long-time rumour says,
as protestation at the system which
demanded rates from everyone, but of
which Nonconformist schools received no share.
No worse for wear, they turned up in a field!

Abraham and Anne Brierley

The issue of Church Rates provoked a long
and argumentative debate which took
the better part of forty years to be
resolved within the nineteenth century.
It's said that Abraham Brierley threatened his
mill workers with the sack if they refused
to cast their vote in favour of this tax;
and Jacob Bright (who's mentioned later on)
was fined for contraventions of this law.

These were contentious times by all accounts!

*The font in St. Mary's Church and stylised drawings
of three of the inlaid stone carvings*

In Reverend Kempthorne's time in eighteen
ninety six, James Brierley died who'd worshipped at
St. Mary's Church for fifty seven years
of married life with Alice by his side.
Their children gave the Lectern in their memory -
a brazen eagle, symbol of St. John.
The Misses Brierley carried on the family's
long connection with St. Mary's Church.

Reverend J.A. Kempthorne (later Bishop of Lichfield)

The old National School, Redcross Street...

...and the new

(Illustrations from 'A Short History of St. Mary's Parish' by Rev. A.R. Langford-Brown.)

The century's end was marked by comment made
by Thomas Meadowcroft, St. Mary's
Parish Clerk - more a complaint - that dirt that once
was but a spittleful amounted to
a bucketful when congregation went!

The Parish building enterprises which
accompanied this growth in popularity
involved a smaller Mission Church
in Whitehall Street; and the enlargement of
the National School on Redcross Street - the first
free school in Rochdale, built eighteen fifteen.
As its Trustees it had the Vicar, several
Royds, and Jonathan Fildes (there's more to tell)
who left the school 'a thousand' in his Will.

A few years later on ... St. Mary's Church
gave cause for fear when noise of splitting timbers,
cracking walls, disturbed the worship on
a Sunday morn, and once again the need
for funds was clear - Miss H. M. Crompton met
two thirds of cost of fifteen thousand pounds.

The stained glass windows from the old church were
re-set, apart from three, when new St. Mary's
Church was built; they're all along the North
wall now, and tell the story of the life
and death of Christ. This church was consecrated
nineteen hundred and eleven: such
a grand occasion with the Bishop in
his scarlet robes, and flowers and leaves were strewn
upon the ground; a week of festival
when many former clergy of the church
returned and no doubt marvelled at the work
of J. N. Comper, architect, whose aim
had been so well-achieved in keeping much
of value from the old church in the new.

*Representations of three of the
stained glass roundels in St. Mary's Church.*

A small section of the carved wooden Rood Screen in St. Mary's Church.

'Apostles with appropriate symbols of their martyrdom or ministry ...'

Part of the Eastern Window in St. Mary's Church.

He was meticulous in his design
of every item in the church down to
ecclesiastical embroidery,
from hand-made Tuckers' bricks outside to the
ornately carved Rood Screen within.
This masterpiece depicting Christ on Calvary
and in Ascended Grace above the twelve
Apostles with appropriate symbols of
their martyrdom or ministry ... absorbs
the gaze ... until it passes through to see
the lovely Eastern Window, which portrays
God's Revelation of Himself to man
from Creation to Ascension - with one
small human touch of Comper's own, which you
can see if you look carefully in the
second window light from right hand side ...
a STRAWBERRY! This he adopted as
his sign because it was his father's way,
when visiting his poor parishioners,
to take some strawberries with him as a treat.

The strawberry 'motif' of Church Architect, Sir J.N. Comper.

St. Mary's Parsonage, eighteen Toad Lane,
first built in seventeen sixty seven, was built
again nineteen-o-five. This fine brick building
standing opposite St. Mary's Place,
no longer is the Vicar's residence.

Although the Brierleys never rose to quite
the same high status as the Royds, their names
appear together on the Wardens' lists
of both St. Mary's and St. Chad's. As
Henry Brierley wrote of eighteen twelve, they shared
their school days at the Rochdale Grammar School
in company with those of "humbler station".

Two schools you'll find on Heights Lane now: the one
built on the site of Royds' 'Brown Hill' still keeps
the name - it's Brownhill Special School (and more
about this subject later on) but back
in seventeen forty, when t'was called Toad Lane,
a school master in Hanging Road was paid
six pounds a year from rent on cottages
in Toad Lane as part of an endowment.
The rent increased in eighteen twenty seven
to twenty four pounds eleven, so further down
Toad Lane a cottage then became a school.
(In Heights Lane days it stood at number five).

At first this school was known as Taylor's
Charity School, because it offered twenty
children who were poor a chance of
education free. The school was much improved
in eighteen forty by a wine merchant's
generosity, and by the year of
eighteen eighty nine listed fifty five
scholars - twenty free and thirty five paid.

The school had Unitarian Trustees,
amongst whom Benjamin and Samuel Heape
belonged to yet another well-known
family. It closed in eighteen ninety one.

The cottages of Taylor's Charity which stood between 'Knowsley Villa' and 'Brown Hill'.

The cottages of Taylor's Charity
stood next to 'Knowsley' and before 'Brown Hill',
if you were going up Heights Lane from town.
The lane in front was only one car's width
until they were demolished, making space.

'Knowsley Villa' wasn't built until
the eighteen seventies, being occupied
in eighteen eighty one by widower,
Luke Collier, Australian by birth;
confectioner's machinist who employed
two boys and twenty men, and had four children
to bring up alone. But its most famous
resident in modern times must be
the gynaecologist and pioneer
of 'test-tube births' named Patrick Steptoe.

It's easy to digress … but back to schools.

The eighteen seventy Education Act
decreed School Boards should supervise the teaching
in the schools, so Board Schools came to be,
including one built eighteen seventy nine
called 'Cronkeyshaw'. It flourishes today
(although the building's an anxiety)
and right from start its "elementary work"
was "exceptionally good". The log book for
the school can tell a story of its own …
of how attendance was affected by
the whooping cough and measles in the eighteen
nineties and how once the school was closed
for three weeks and a day because of this.
And how in nineteen hundred on the twenty
first of May, the children sang the National
Anthem outside on the Common, and gave
three cheers for Queen Victoria and
Colonel Baden Powell - then were given a
holiday, perhaps to join their parents
on that brass band march all round the town, for
Mafeking's Relief was such a victory!

Joseph Brierley, J.P. Castleton, (James
Brierley's brother - Abraham's son) was
elected to the first School Board, and so
was Henry Brierley later on; the log
bears witness to their visits in this role.

Cronkeyshaw School and Common. See Map p4
At this point old Toad Lane ended and the packhorse route turned off via Casson Gate to Syke and Brown Wardle. Also in view, the trees of Falinge Park, and Bench Carr next to Bent Meadows. (See text p96 for discussion of names.)

It's right that part of old Toad Lane has been
conserved, but much is lost of what it was
when woollen merchants walked the street. The town
first had a woollen trade in thirteenth century
times, and weavers of the sixteen hundreds
thrived on cottage looms until the seventeen
sixties 'Revolution' came, and families
like the Royds grew rich on manufacturing.

Yes, eighteen hundred saw the boom, with Toad
Lane woollen market bringing merchants in
on horseback from Bradford, Halifax and
Haslingden to patronise their favourite
Lord Street inns (though at the time it was
Blackwater Street). 'The Clock Face' and 'The Coach'
deserved to be conserved, and 'Griffin', 'King's Head',
'Saddle', 'White Horse', 'White Bear', 'Red Lion',
all did good trade on both sides of the street.

The kind of service offered by these inns
with 'well-aired beds' and stabling is shown
on this account from 'Tweedale's', Baillie Street.

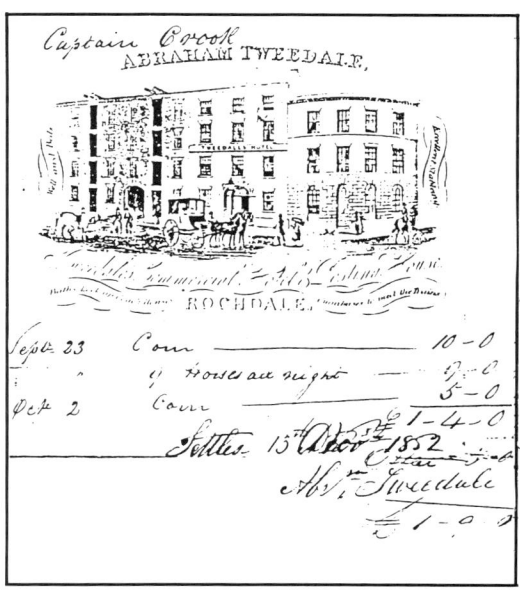

(From D. Freedman's collection)
See Map p11

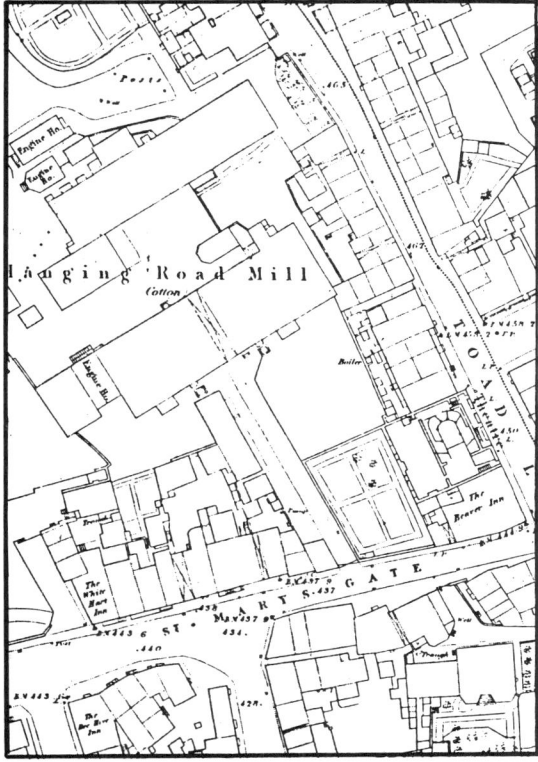

Plan of Hanging Road Cotton Mill reproduced from 1851 O.S. Map.

Then, as the nineteenth century's seeds were sown, those cotton mills sprang up all over town!

Joseph Brierley, Henry's grandfather,
became a partner, late in his career,
in one of town's first cotton mills in
Hanging Road, built seventeen ninety five about;
and Abraham Brierley later owned it too.

This mill, or part of it's still there. If you
just cross St. Mary's Gate and follow Toad Lane
through, both Hanging Road and Toad Lane are
unmarked, but Hanging Road goes through to
Ormerods, the label specialists, who have
the first block of the mill in tact, and straight
ahead is Sharples' 'Waljan' Mill, which is
the part still standing of the second block
seen on the plan of the original mill.

This firm's been there since nineteen forty eight.
It started up in silk, and now is one
of three remaining 'throwsters' in the whole
of Lancashire. Still moving with the times,
its yarns, synthetics too, are used for things
like hosepipes, underwear and parachutes.

Ormerods Limited (Printers) occupy the first block of the former Hanging Road Cotton Mill.

Jacob Bright

John Bright

A Quaker gentleman called Jacob Bright
once lived at seventy two Toad Lane; reports
do say he started as a weaver at
the cotton mill in Hanging Road, eighteen-o-two -
although John Bright himself gave this
as date when cotton mill was built, and said
his father helped to set machinery up,
(the owners, John and William Holme, were friends)
then took the cloth to market and made sure
the invoices were promptly sent. But then
in eighteen hundred and nine, Jacob moved
to 'Greenbank', Cronkeyshaw, to build his mills -
one burnt to bits; and two years on was when
young John was born ... to be a famous man.

The story of John Bright's another tale ...
his fight against the Corn Laws and his
parliamentary career ... it's all been told.
But history shows that Jacob Bright was more
benevolent than any of his sons
when times were hard and workers were laid off.
And did you know that John Bright's Fieldhouse Mills
wove carpets too in eighteen forty nine?

*Left: **The remaining part of the second block of the former Hanging Road Cotton Mill.
View of W. & J. Sharples' 'Waljan' Mill from the back.***

It seems strange now, but in those times a man's
entitlement to vote depended on
the value of his property - so views
of ordinary folk and those who rented
homes were never represented then,
until the franchise was extended.

Locally, this happened eighteen fifty three
but not for over sixty years in
national affairs - and this was one thing that
the Chartists wanted changed. So poverty
and powerlessness resulted in a charged,
explosive atmosphere within the town
whilst 'industry' was taking root, with strikes,
and riots quelled by military force.

The Shuttle Riots, eighteen-o-eight, provide
a useful focal point for study now,
because the mill owners, the weavers and
St. Mary's Church were all involved. The way
it started was like this: the hand loom weavers
for the cotton mills disputed with
the owners - Midgley's mill at Buersil,
Robert Holt's of Well i'th' Lane and James Royds'
mill at Oakenrod - about the rates
of pay which fell below the level they'd
agreed. The weavers took away the shuttles
from the looms to stop production, and
they hid them, several cart loads, at the top
of old Blackwater Street. The shuttles were
retrieved by the authorities, then locked
in Rope Street jail. The weavers set the jail
on fire when efforts to reclaim them failed.

It's said that nearly every shop in Yorkshire
Street had windows broken in the riots.
Mill owners were attacked, including Royds
on Toad Lane near his home. The Riot Act
was read - a thousand soldiers drafted in
from Halifax to stamp it out. (Rochdale's
own band of 'Volunteers' had been discharged.)
They billeted the soldiers in the church,
with borrowed bedding bolstering the pews,
and in the pubs and Cloth Hall near at hand.

The riot was suppressed and weavers had
no choice but to return to work without
a penny increase on their wages won.
Their weekly wage was fifteen shillings then.
Of course, the wages issue lingered on!

The six points of the People's Charter as summarised on a broadsheet. The Charter was published as a draft parliamentary bill on 8th May 1938.

1
A VOTE
for every man twenty-one years of age, of sound mind, and not undergoing punishment for crime.

2
THE BALLOT
to protect the elector in the exercise of his vote.

3
NO PROPERTY QUALIFICATION
for Members of Parliament — thus enabling the constituencies to return the man of their choice, be he rich or poor.

4
PAYMENT OF MEMBERS
thus enabling an honest tradesman, working man, or other person, to serve a constituency, when taken from his business to attend to the interests of the Country.

5
EQUAL CONSTITUENCIES
securing the same amount of representation for the same number of electors, instead of allowing small constituencies to swamp the votes of large ones.

6
ANNUAL PARLIAMENTS
thus presenting the most effectual check to bribery and intimidation, since though a constituency might be bought once in seven years (even with the ballot), no purse could buy a constituency (under a system of universal suffrage) in each ensuing twelve-month; and since members, when elected for a year only, would not be able to defy and betray their constituents as now.

(Source: 'Chartism and Society' Ed. F.C. Mather)

And sometimes force was used without due cause …
From Rochdale, Middleton and round about,
six thousand radicals with banners raised
and marching bands and song, and laurel branches
held in youthful hands, walked all the way
with Samuel Bamford in the lead, to hear
their national leader, Hunt, address a peaceful
crowd of sixty thousand strong. Patrols
of Connaught Rangers lined the route (who came
from Rochdale's Summercastle barracks) to
make sure the crowd was orderly. The year
was eighteen nineteen, August, and the place
St. Peter's Fields in Manchester. The Riot
Act was read before the meeting was
'dispersed' by order of the County Justice,
Reverend William Hay, who shortly was
rewarded for this 'public service' by
appointment here as Vicar of St. Chad's.
Time has not vindicated him! Within
ten minutes of the start, the cavalry
and infantry just mowed them down. It's since
been called 'The Massacre of Peterloo'.

And those of Jacob Bright's employees who
were on that march returned to Cronkeyshaw
that night to tell how they'd escaped the wrath.
It's said John Bright, just eight years old, looked on
at their distress "with wonder-waiting eyes".

The homely lifestyles of the cottage weavers
disappeared when competition from
the factories came and many went to work
in mills to make ends meet, but weavers feared
they'd lose their jobs when power looms came in
(although this fear was somewhat premature)
and riots broke out again in eighteen twenty
nine - this time resulting in the loss
of lives. And then, when in the thirties textile
prices slumped, so wages did. How many
shillings did they earn in eighteen thirty
four? Just five or six per week. 'The Hungry
Forties' they were called; long working hours
from dawn to dusk and little more than mounting
debt to show for it, and many sacked.

For many, life was short and desperate.

The mills employed the children and their mothers
rather than the men and turnover
was high. The figures from the mill of
Abraham Brierley, eighteen fifty one, reveal
five hundred and twenty five employed
that year (three hundred jobs about) - just eighty
two were men, with nearly twice that number
women, and the rest were boys and girls.

Right: Illustration from 'Peterloo 1819 – Portfolio of Contemporary Documents', Manchester Local History Library.

So, when you see the 'quaint' Toad Lane the town
has now, remember how it echoed once
to clog-clad men and women on their way
to rousing gatherings on Cronkeyshaw;
with soldiers' boots heard often close behind.

REDUCTION OF WAGES!

NOTICE,

THAT THERE WILL BE A

Public Meeting,

OF ALL WOOLLEN

Weavers and Spinners,

HELD ON CRONKEYSHAW,

On Tuesday next the 15th Instant, at One o'Clock in the Afternoon.

To take into consideration the inconsistent Conduct of the Woollen Manufacturers generally, in consequence of their unparalleled, and again uncalled for Reduction of Wages, which must inevitably drive us all to a state of Pauperism, Degradation, and Starvation, once so foreign to Englishmen and Britons, and at the same time to adopt Measures to make a stand against such Arbitrary, Ruinous, and various Contrivances, to which they resort to abridge the Wages of our Labour, and those comforts which are even essentially necessary to sustain Life itself.

It is therefore presumed that all *Weavers and Spinners*, having nothing to depend upon but the Woollen Trade, or that wish not to reap benefits at the expense of their Neighbours, or who consider *their All now to be at Stake*, will attend the said MEETING, and endeavour to prove to the Country, that to reduce us from the STATEMENT PRICES of 1824, is reducing us below the level of *Brute Beasts*, and a bare subsistence, and thereby thrusting us out from the pale of Society.

THE CHAIR TO BE TAKEN AT ONE o'CLOCK.

BY ORDER OF THE COMMITTEE.

Rochdale, May 8th, 1827.

J. WESTALL, PRINTER, STATIONER, &c. 5, NEW-MARKET, ROCHDALE.

Why was it that the Co-op Movement started
in these times? Well, broadly speaking, it
arose from practical necessity -
the need of working folk to overcome
their exploitation by the mill shops and
the local shopkeepers who falsified
the weights of food and mixed in 'other'
substances - and from a combination of
the Chartist and the Owenite philosophies
which sought a fair deal for the 'honest
working man', the first through Parliamentary
Reform (with factions advocating use
of force); the second through the visionary
ideals of Robert Owen, who had ideas
to set up whole 'co-operative'
communities on self-sufficient lines.
Though, paradoxically, he wasn't very keen
on retail Co-op shops at first.

A Social Hall was opened by the
followers of Robert Owen right opposite
St. James's Church in eighteen thirty eight.

Another 'father' of the Movement and
supporter of the Rochdale Pioneers
was G. J. Holyoake, whose writings spread
the message far and wide across the world.

Robert Owen

The local leaders who subscribed to these
ideals of radical reform were men
like Thomas Livsey and James Taylor and
James Leach. It's not disputed Thomas Livsey
had enormous influence on Rochdale
politics within the nineteenth century,
but maybe his connection with Toad Lane
before he moved to Well i'th' Lane is worth
a mention too. He was a blacksmith and
a publican. His inn 'The Three Horse Shoes'
was later known as 'Fox and Dog' - the forge,
next-door-but-three. James Taylor? Methodist
hat manufacturer of Spotland Bridge.

There's little doubt that Thomas Livsey and
his Chartist friends did take initial steps
to start the Rochdale Pioneers, announcing
their intentions in 'The Guardian'
on third December eighteen forty two.

And so, among the flannel weavers, joiners,
shoemakers and wool sorters; the clogger,
warper, hawker, slubber, hatter,
warehouseman and stationery engineer
and others who made up the twenty eight
first members of the Toad Lane Pioneers,
there were eight Chartists, fourteen Socialists,
a Congregationalist and Unitarians.

Thomas Livsey

Though politics and church had neutral roles
within the Pioneers' affairs, this was
a working class and Nonconformist venture
nonetheless ... which started with a twopenny
donation every week until enough
was saved to rent the ground floor of a warehouse
in Toad Lane, and what was left was spent
on oatmeal, butter, sugar, flour and candles.

They opened in the evenings first, but prices
which were fair attracted trade and soon
they opened in the day; and later had
a Library and Reading Room upstairs,
and Women's Guild in eighteen eighty three.

The Co-op shops gave working folk control
of their affairs - they prospered well on
principles of profit-sharing dividend ...
and now across the world they've wholesale,
retail, travel, banking and insurance,
politics and education all in hand.

Is this what dreamer Robert Owen planned?

On the right, towards the bottom of Toad Lane.
Thomas Livsey's smithy was at the opposite end of the block
from his inn.
See Map p11.

Toad Lane had strong connections, not just with
wool and cotton, but felt and flannel too,
and in the seventeen seventies had a trade
in hats unrivalled in the world perhaps -
a trade which started fifteen eighty six.

The sum of thirty thousand pounds was owed
to Jonathan Fildes in seventeen seventy five,
when England and America fought the War
of Independence (which *they* won), and he
was paid in silver bars and bullion ...
but only after thirty years had passed!

Two kinds of hat were made to bring this trade.
The owners of the slaves wore beaver-covered
felt with twelve-inch sun-shade brims; the slaves
wore felt upon their heads, in colours to
distinguish them from other owners' slaves.

It's known the felt was dyed and hats were made
at 'Hatter's Stove' where 'Water House' was built
(across and left from 'Waljan' Mill). And there's
a mill in School Street - owned by Wear Fine now
and previously by Taylors (Engineers) -
built eighteen fifty six on land which Edmund
Howard, cotton spinner, bought from Fildes'
'inheritance'. The area round there
was always known as Waterhouses then.
The 'White Horse' in Blackwater Street and other
property belonged to Fildes, as well
as farms at Wardle, Syke and Blackstone Edge.

Mill on School Street/Waterhouse Street built c.1856.

Houses on Toad Lane c.1930 including 'Water House', another Fildes' residence. (See Map p73)

The Fildes' stone mansion 'Quarry Hill', where
Jonathans of several generations lived
(and artist Edward Stott was born in eighteen
fifty nine) was in the posh half of
Toad Lane, not far from the Infirmary
(built eighteen thirty one) which profited
from Fildes' great wealth as other causes did.
The house, long since divided into two,
still stands mysteriously within walled grounds.

The large stone house next door, right next to the
Infirmary and called 'Stone Hill', was built
much later, round about the time this part
of Toad Lane was re-named Heights Lane; and owned
in eighteen sixty one by one James Pilling,
member of the family of cotton
spinners of that name who were among
the first to introduce this trade to town.

Views of 'Quarry Hill' built c.1692.

'Stone Hill' built c.1860.

'Quarry Hill' was built over half a century before Toad Lane became a Turnpike Road, and is almost certainly the oldest property along this route.

Edwin Waugh, born 1817 — a pupil of the National School, Redcross Street.

So much has changed around the town end of Toad Lane, and now there's nothing left to show that cottages were there or 'Th'Old Clock Face', once famous Edwin Waugh's birthplace, except a plaque which marks the spot right opposite the new Co-op inside the shopping precinct. This lad, whose father was a shoemaker, became a dialect poet of great renown.

There have been several other Co-ops on Toad Lane - best known, the Central Pioneers which opened eighteen sixty seven and stood its ground about a hundred years; and that was built upon the site a Theatre stood from seventeen ninety three or thereabouts to eighteen sixty five. The diary of stage carpenter reveals how popular was 'Shakespeare' in the town. Sam Brierley and his brothers played supporting roles to the professionals in many a play; and all the cast were welcomed at the inn, the 'Woolpack' off Toad Lane, where Joseph Brierley and John, his son, were landlords in their time.

Apparently the theatre had some boxes which were much like wooden pews in eighteen fifty nine. It's also where the great composer, Liszt, performed for just one night.

The Central Pioneers on Toad Lane and St. Mary's Gate, built on the site of 'The Beaver Inn' and the Toad Lane Theatre. The shops in the foreground stood opposite St. Mary's Vicarage.

Some gentlemen already mentioned now
crop up again: Jon. Fildes of Quarry Hill
was owner of this Theatre for a while,
along with a consortium of Royds
and other notables. Together with
some cottages, it cost nine hundred pounds.

And eighteen thirty was the year when folk
in town were asked to cast aside 'the drink'.
The 'Temperance Cause' was introduced on stage
by Reverend Crookshank at the invitation
of John Bright and others of like mind.
The Quakers, Baptists, Methodists and all …
all soberly agreed on abstinence.

Just four years later on in eighteen thirty
four, R. Shuttleworth presided at
a meeting of a different kind held at
'The Old Clock Face', and John and Jacob Bright
were there as founder members of the new
Reform Association (Liberal).

The 'Coach and Horses' inn next door had links
with Rochdale's working class, and both the
Radical and Liberal Reformers used
the Theatre in Toad Lane to stage debate.

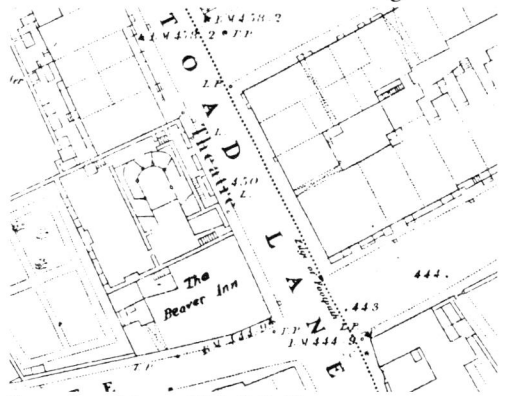

Reproduced from 1851 O.S. Map

Before the Toad Lane Theatre was set up,
the building there was used for Wesleyans
to meet in prayer. In fact, John Wesley preached
on April twenty ninth in seventeen seventy
(often then for seventeen years) but died
before the Chapel moved to Union Street.

When this took place in seventeen ninety three,
a little Sunday School had found a home.
James Hamilton had started it in seventeen
eighty two. He was a tin-plate worker
living in Blackwater Street, who took
the children to three services in turn,
the Unitarians' ... St. Mary's ... and
the Wesleyans', with whom they settled down!

Which brings to mind that church clock of St. Chad's
was made in seventeen eighty nine by one
John Barnish of Toad Lane. It chimed a lot -
a different tune for each day of the week!
It played 'Lovely Nancy' on a Monday
and 'Life let us cherish' on a Tuesday,
with different Psalms for Friday and Sunday.
The chimes rang out till eighteen sixty five.

John Barnish too was present on the day
when innocents were killed at 'Peterloo'.

But that, indeed, was long ago, and now
there's little left to show of old Toad Lane,
except in library photographs which chart
the decades' demolition and the change.

Rochdale Parish Church, St. Chad's, with chiming clock (1789-1865).

Perhaps it's time to have a rest from facts -
time to reflect and fantasise ... and so
if you have time to stop and sit in new
St. Mary's Place or take the chance to see
St. Mary's Church nearby, whose stone interior
and colonnades create an ambience
of olden days, you might just sense
the *feeling* of Toad Lane, and let your mind
become attuned to times now past to which
the tales and truths which follow do belong.

The first of these, still talked about today,
goes back to fourteenth century times, when
Rochdale was called Rachedale, but Oakley who
records the tale prefers the spelling
'Rachedall'; and for reasons given later
in this poem, the area round St. Mary's
and Toad Lane is referred to as The Baum.
The narrow entrance to the narrow street
that bore the name is still on Yorkshire Street.

St. Mary's Place, now part of the Conservation Area, once enclosed small businesses and workshops, including a Shirt Factory. (See Map p65)

St. Mary's Church built 1742
(The Baum Chapel)

When moonlight dances on the churchyard stones,
a ghostly rabbit haunts St. Mary's walls.
Sometimes burrowing in the ancient mould,
or brushing whiskers in an upright pose.
All plump and white and far too quick for those
'brave' men who used to try to kill with guns,
Jig Billy and Bill Dowfin and the rest;
or others who confounded it in verse,
entreating dogs to "worry, toss and tease".

In truth - if truth there is - the rabbit's tale
speaks more of love and of the fairies' powers
than deeds of horror in the Chapel's grounds;
though, truthfully, the Black Death plagued the land.
The handsome Earl of Oxford's mission was
to save his loved one, Blanche, the sister
of Rachedall's Vicar, Thomas de Boulton,
though nearness of blood forbade their union.

The Earl of Oxford's costume

*And so, the story goes, there is a stone
on Whitworth moors by which the Earl lay down
to rest and eat, and there two Rachedall lads
came by, surprised to find this grandee from
the third King Edward's court, and doffed their caps.
Their rustic eyes looked on a man of strange
attire, ridiculous high fashion such
that, it is said, the fairies rocked with laughter
as they danced, and left misshapen rings
for country folk to find and wonder at.*

*The Earl was fair of face with long beard trimmed
with care, and on his head a silken hood,
close-fitting bonnet buttoned under chin;
be-jewelled embroidered fabled beasts it showed.
Beneath his coat - half white, half purple - trousers
barely reached the middle of his thighs, and
stockinged legs - one blue, one red - disported
long pointed shoes which fastened to his knees
by silver chains. No wonder fairies mocked!*

'But from the East the mist it came ...'

But now to serious matters ... so the Earl
enquired: "There is no sickness in these parts?"
A nervous lad replied he knew of none
but what fell to the common lot of men.
"What of Rachedall? Any stir of terror there?"
None that they knew of, was their shocked reply.
In West Yorkshire, the Earl knew all too well,
the plague had spread ... but Blanche seemed safe awhile.
And so he gave them money for their news
and slept ... but from the East the mist it came,
shaped like a mighty vengeful angel with
a great whip ... and Rachedall in its path.

It passed ... the night was blackly-bright with stars.
The Earl had slept too long, but then awoke.
Circling the stone in merry dance were elves,
sparkling green and silver in the moonglow,
singing as they skipped a silly little song.
With gleaming eyes and beating wings, a small
elf played the fiddle, cross-legged on the stone.
"Cease!" said the Fairy Queen. "Have you no care
for the fate befalling Rachedall?" The Earl
she gave one wish to write upon the stone
the name of one to save – perhaps himself?

His diamond ring was hard as glass and with
it he did scratch the letters roughly, but
as he wrote the name of Blanche, in a flash
blinding to the eyes, a white rabbit sat
upon the stone, a gold band round its neck.
And playing cards were lying by its side –
the earliest of their kind, not known to him.
Four suits: rabbits, roses, pinks and columbine;
and there upon the Queen of Rabbits' card
appeared the face of Blanche. What could it mean?
That Blanche must have the rabbit to protect
her from the plague ... or so the Earl believed.

He made his way on foot, his horse being lame ...
Time to ponder on the quirk of fate that
made him love a girl he could not marry;
in fact, a girl he had not seen for years ...
Better that they'd never loved at all?

He found Blanche and her brother at their home,
where she was weak and fevered with the plague.
Yet when she took the rabbit from the Earl,
it was as though a surge of health rushed through;
and she survived to help her brother tend
the sick, the rabbit always by her side.

The Earl helped too, for there was much distress,
especially in 'The Baum' where people lived
all closely housed in wooden rows, but when
he caught the dread disease - which ran its course
in just three days - his life was somehow spared.
Yet 'half of England' died with tortured lungs
and skin and tongue all blackened, hence the name.
So many clergy met their deaths this way,
and, sad to say, Thomas de Boulton died,
Feast of St. Matthew, thirteen forty nine.
In truth, the plague was spread by rats not mist,
by sufferers, not thin air - we know this now.

The rabbit disappeared the day the plague
had claimed its awful toll ... yet folk do swear
it did return, though bear in mind there was
no Chapel nor a graveyard in The Baum
until four centuries on - St. Mary's, founded
seventeen forty two. And that's a fact!

This story comes from times gone by when folk
believed in fairies' powers, so only if
you secretly still do, perchance you'll catch
a fleeting glimpse of rabbit's paws and golden
band near Whitworth's 'Monstone' on the moors.
And here's another ending to the tale ...
If balm herb grew as once it surely did
among the graves, the moonshine's mischief could play tricks,
and turn those snow-white fairy flowers to rabbits' tails!

Balm herb

'Four suits: rabbits, roses, pinks and columbine ...'

Copyright reserved: Published in 1989 as part of 'Toad Lane to The Heights'. ISBN 0 9514563 1 8

Postscript …

*It's odd how nick names come to be, but this
one of 'Baum Rabbit' - perhaps a little
cruel but also very apt - was given to
the Parish Clerk who followed Robert
Schofield in eighteen fifty five; his name
was Thomas Nield, a little wizened man,
who chased off beggars and the local lads.*

*He proved especially elusive when
the cleaning wasn't to the liking of
the Wardens, saying, "Well, you know that I
can't see … or hear" … and "I'm rheumatic!" too.
"At any rate," one Warden said, "it seems
that he can feel!" But when the Reverend
Napier Sharpe came on the scene in eighteen
sixty six, they just did not see eye to eye.
The Vicar asked him not to wear his clogs
in church, so Thomas bought an even noisier
pair of boots … and then was pensioned off!*

Another tale, much less well-known, but one
which too dates back to fourteenth century times,
concerns the policy of Edward Third
to foster woollen manufacturing
in England by inviting Flemish cloth
experts to settle here and teach their craft.
It's said some came to Rochdale, dwelling in
the western part of town, and that again
in fifteen seventy six some more arrived.

But nothing in the Parish Registers
of sixteen hundreds proves the point, and two
reliable historians discount
the 'facts' as mere embroidered myth ... which makes
it puzzling why we have such names as 'Baum',
which could mean 'trees or grove', and 'tod', which could
mean 'death'; and mill names such as Mardyke and
Dunkirk, although the latter do not date
from earlier than the eighteenth century,
both now adorning flats in College Bank.

Another explanation for these two
particular names is that green baize was sent
to Moordyke (Holland) and Dunkirk as part
of Rochdale's export trade. The same applies
to Holland Street (and Mill and Rise) although
Charles Holland had a chandler's business there.
Perhaps his name was given to the street?

*Left: Reproduced from
the 1851 Ordnance Survey Map.*

Coincidence, d'you think? The links with 'tod'
(in either connotation, 'wool' or 'death')
might just seem less convincing than the links
with toads as far as Toad Lane's name's concerned.
But there will always be a nagging doubt
when Deeds which date from sixteen ninety five
refer to Thomas Ffylds (the Fildes of
'Quarry Hill') as dyer of 'TOD' Lane ... but then
it's also worth remembering that spelling
then was all too often 'all t' pot'!

And as to 'Baum' ... a widely held belief
is that the local way of saying 'balm'
is how the area got its name, because
there is no doubt that balm herb grew on
meadowland whose later use was for St. Mary's
graves, and went on popping up between
the stones. (Perhaps it kept some rabbits fit!)

This plant was gathered by the local folk
(white mint prepared as salve or balm) and in
the year of seventeen ninety could be bought
with other herbal remedies at
Mally o'Doctor's place; she praised the balm
and said: "Tha mun stick to it mon - an' th'all
soon be o'reet!" 'Baum-tay' was yet another
way of taking this medicinal herb.

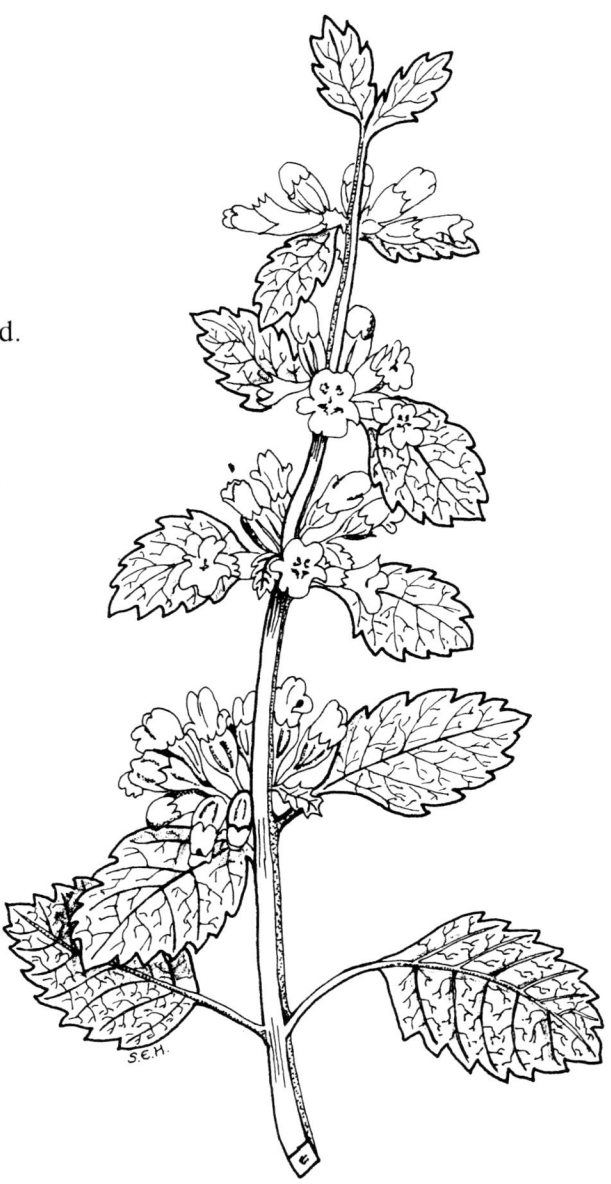

'Melissa Officinalis' or Balm

There have been other ghosts to walk The Baum.
In recent times before the seventies
shopping centre redevelopment began –
witnesses to both a woman and a man.

The woman, in Victorian dress, was often
heard and sometimes seen in Woolworth's store.
The first floor stockroom turned an icy chill,
between the household goods and birthday cards,
before she did appear ... yet no harm meant.

The man who walked The Baum at night came from
an earlier time, was dressed in Middle Ages
garb by all accounts, and wandered from
the churchyard, not in direct line, but through
the market wall towards the fish ... then through
the stalls towards the open market, where
he disappeared at last in the canteen.
Remember now, this too was as it was
before the planners modernised the town.
So life-like did he look that policemen on
the beat would note him in their little books!

Reproduced from the 1930 Ordnance Survey Map.

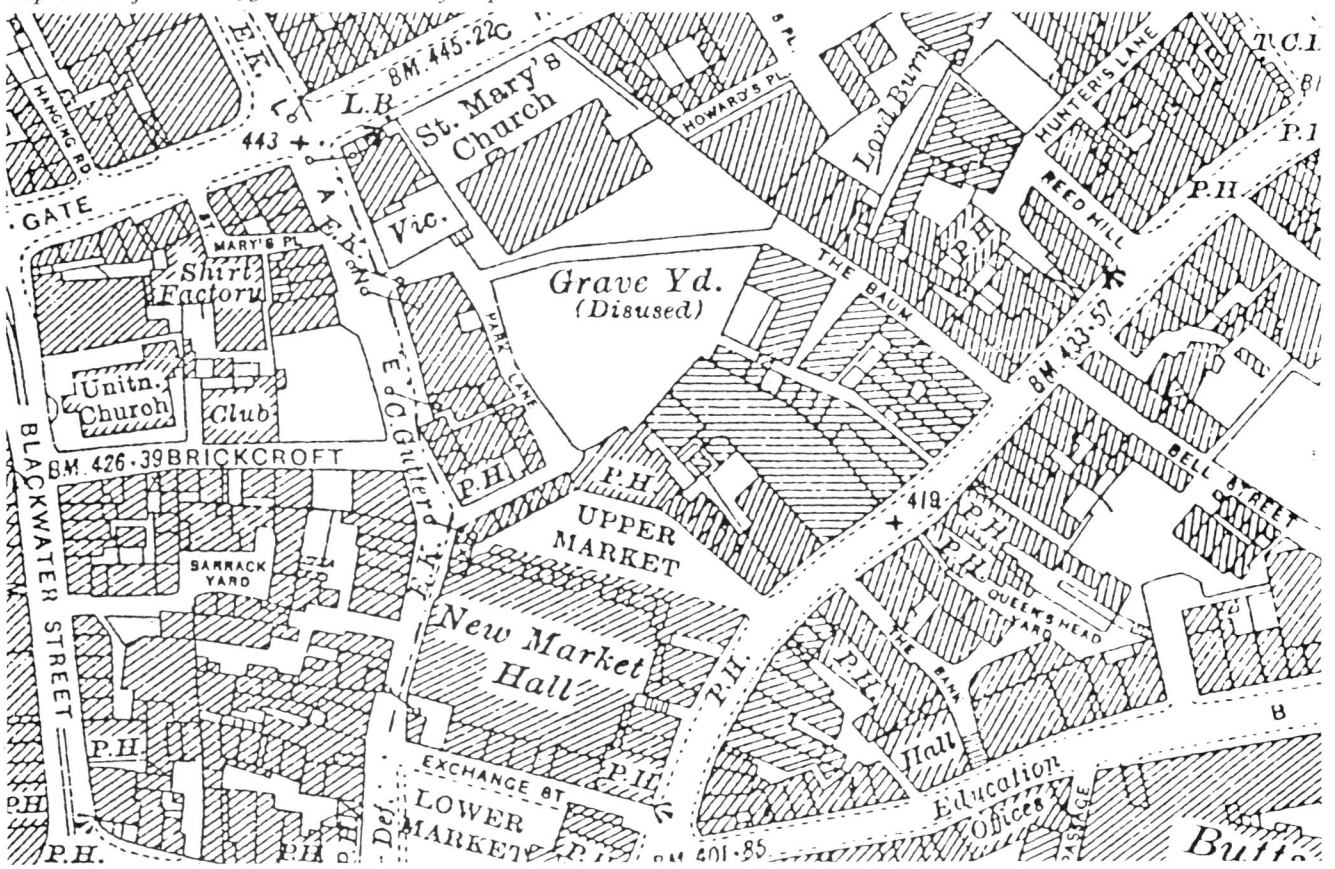

And there's a ghost that haunts 'Brownhill Hotel'.
He wears a hat, check shirt and thick cord trousers,
(rather casual dresser - for a ghost!)
and has been seen most in the area of
the toilets - somewhat strange, until you know
that this is where the staircase used to be,
from which, it's said, a man once hanged himself.
THOSE staircase spindles decorate the bar.

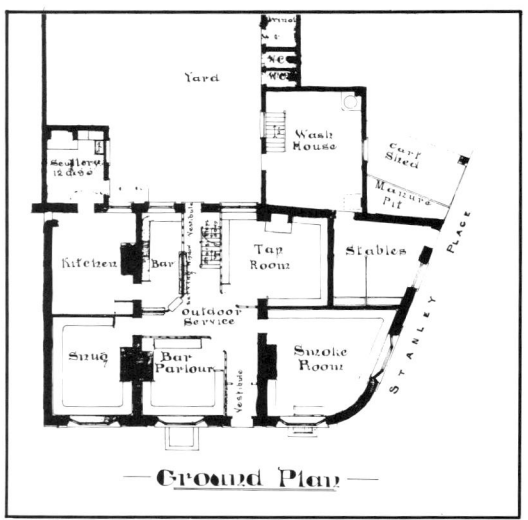

Peter and Kathleen Coleman, landlord and landlady of 'The Brownhill Hotel' 1988 — the only surviving pub from old Toad Lane.

Brown Hill Hotel,
Heights Lane, Rochdale.

PROPRIETOR - ELLIS SMITH.

A Grand Open Show of
WORKING HOMER PIGEONS
Will be held at the above house,
On Saturday, Dec. 8th, and following day.

FIRST PRIZE, 10/-; SECOND, 5/-; THIRD, 2/6.
PRIZE MONEY GUARANTEED.
SPECIAL PRIZES IN EVERY CLASS.

Class 1—Flying Homer Cock, bred previous to 1906
Class 2—Flying Homer Hen,   ,,   ,,   ,,
Class 3—Flying Homer Cock, bred in 1906 to be rung
Class 4—Flying Homer Hen,   ,,   ,,   ,,
Class 5—Flying Homer Cock, bred in 1906, to have flown 60 miles
Class 6—Flying Homer Hen,   ,,   ,,   ,,
Class 7—Likeliest Bird, Cock, for short distance
Class 8—Likeliest Bird, Hen,   ,,   ,,

ENTRY FEE, 1/- PER BIRD.
Entries Close Thursday, December 6th, 1906.

Judge, Working Homers, MR. H. BILSBOROUGH,
The Successful Alderley Edge and Manchester Dis. Federation Fancier.

Judge, Short Distance, MR. ROBERT ASPLEY,
Of 19, Toad Lane, Rochdale.

ADMISSION BY CATALOGUE.
Wines, Ales, and Spirits of the Best Quality. Choice Cigars.
Show Room Two Minutes Walk from the Market.

HOWARD, PRINTER, WHITWORTH.

(Source of plan and catalogue: A. Edwards)

This pub's been there since eighteen twenty six
at least - the rings to tether horses to
were found embedded in the plastered walls.
You'll see the stables on the plan which shows
the lay-out up until this century.

The landlord when the pub was 'modernised'
nineteen-o-five was Ellis Smith, who liked
a crowd about the place: from pigeon fanciers ...
to fifty of the local children he
invited to a party, but was told
politely by the constables that this
was not allowed on licensed premises.

One old connection with the house 'Brown Hill' is that the Fishwick family were once its residents; the chief rent for the pub was paid to them when leasehold rights were sold in eighteen seventy seven. Which Fishwicks lived there? Jane and Henry Halliwell - a land surveyor and the head of H. H. Fishwick (Colliery Proprietors) and Co., in partnership with Albert Hudson Royds, who lived at 'Falinge Lawn', Bent Meadows then.

H. H. was also friend and Warden to the Reverend Inchbald at St. Mary's Church, and Tory Council Representative for Spotland Ward in eighteen fifty seven. The son of Henry Halliwell is now remembered as the Henry Fishwick who bequeathed as accurate a 'History of Rochdale' as you'll find. He too was on the Council and elected to the first School Board. He lived at 'Carr Hill' many years, then moved up to 'The Heights'; and otherwise the Fishwicks had a Broker's business in Blackwater Street ... just one more family whose lives revolved around this ancient route.

Top: Jane Fishwick, wife of Henry Halliwell Fishwick.
Bottom: Colonel Henry Fishwick, historian.
(Top: from 'A Genealogical Memorial of the Fishwick Family' by Henry Fishwick.)
See p14 re 'Brown Hill'.

Albert Hudson Royds, eldest son of Clement Royds. Robbed by highwaymen at Slattocks on 24th September 1835.

The house 'Brown Hill' was quite unusual - a rambling mansion, no room square and each a different level from the next; outside a striking clock, with scarlet-coated little man, 'Old Tom'; and on the roof a small observatory for looking at the stars.

It had a unique armoury collected by the Royds, and rumour had it that a secret passage led from this room to the town. It stood at least three hundred years before its demolition half way through this century, but back in nineteen twenty two the Corporation bought it for an Open Air School; other buildings were erected in the grounds and subsequent additions and improvements have resulted in the Special School that's there today.

A former pupil, Peter Moros, and
the Head Boy there in nineteen sixty nine,
remembers the importance of the football
team, in spite of asthma - and 'the rest';
and, by his own admission, he was not
so much a 'goody' as a lad who'd dunk
the bullies in the fish pond when he could!

He used to catch the school bus from the town
which went up Blackwater ... St. Mary's Gate
(until the dual carriageway was made
in nineteen sixty four) ... up Hudson Street
and then up Heights Lane to the school.
(Blackwater Street had been the tramway route,
which opened nineteenth June, nineteen-o-two,
because Toad Lane had always been too steep.)
And from the bus he saw the shops with which
he now associates the different stages
in his youth; and stopped on his way home.

He was, he says, a lad with pockets full
of worms and feathers in his hair, who used
to gawp at fishing rods and other things
he couldn't afford in 'Towers' - whilst saving for
a catapult at 'one and six' with which
to flick his bread-and-maggot-balls onto
the water for the fish in Heybrook stream.

Peter Moros in 1969

Then ... pigeons roosting in the rafters of
the shops and warehouses around Toad Lane
mysteriously turned up in young lads' garden
lofts all over town! He breeds them still.

Then ... in his teens the 'Mods and Rockers' craze
was in, and old Miss Bailey's leather shop
at number seventeen Blackwater Street
sold studs for decorating Rockers' gear.
Reluctantly, he had to play at being
a Mod because a Vespa One-Two-Five
was so much cheaper than a motorbike.

The 'Clock Face' and the other pubs provided
lessons about adult life! It's all
gone now, that part of town, yet not what it
all meant ... to different people, different things.
But 'Brownhill' lads today can't have the same
sense of the link between Heights Lane and town.

Brownhill Special School 1988

Blackwater Street early 1960s with St. Mary's Gate at the top.
Photo: A. Marshall

The shop at twenty seven Blackwater Street
was rented back in nineteen thirty seven
by Joseph Towers and newly-married wife
to live in - he was unemployed - and then
their dog had puppies which they put into
the window to be sold. There proved to be
a need for pet food too: that's how the firm
first started, branching into sporting goods
like fishing rods and guns. And now the shop's
on Whitworth Road, the business being owned
by Allan Marshall, local expert on
the area's countryside and amateur
historian, who (coincidentally)
has links with Toad Lane going back to when
his grandmother lived there ... but that's not all.

He made a photographic record of
the area where Abbey Street, Redcross
and Hope Street formed a square with Toad Lane on
one side, and in the middle Hannah's Yard.
The property was built round eighteen fifty
(some of it on land where Fildes made hats)
and must have been quite decent at the start.
The terraced rows and back-to-backs in this
'Mount Pleasant' area resulted in
a densely populated spot which came
to be the Irish quarter of the town.

View from Toad Lane down Abbey Street...

...along Redcross Street

...and down Hope Street (early 1960s)

Photos: A. Marshall

The Irish immigration in the eighteen
forties, prompted by potato famine
and rebellion and destitution
on a massive scale, resulted in
this settlement round Hope Street, Howard Street
and Wilkinson's Yard. Three hundred and three
arrived from Ireland, and by eighteen fifty
one the census shows another thirty
seven children born; and six had gained
an English spouse. Of over seventy
who worked as mill hands, about half were under
sixteen years of age - the youngest child
called Thady Tinsey was eleven years.

The Factory Act of eighteen thirty three
said children from the age of nine could be
employed. Just up the road in John Bright's mills
near Cronkeyshaw, the weekly children's rate
was 'six and three', with sixteen shillings paid
to adult men - this for a ten hour day.
But, unlike most, the Brights provided schools
for workers and their children; and John Bright
was known to be familiar with the Irish
situation and to sympathise.

The Post Office at the corner of Toad Lane and Hope Street was No. 72 — Jacob Bright's home 1802-9.
Reproduced from the 1890 Ordnance Survey Map.

The growing railway network needed labour
too, and twenty nine were so employed.
The first steam locomotive engine puffed
through Rochdale Station twenty sixth of April
eighteen thirty nine. The track was laid
as far as Littleborough on the route
from Manchester to Leeds by then, and you
could stand up in an open truck for 'one
and six' to Manchester - the Third Class rate;
the seats were for the First and Second Class!

The Rochdale-Whitworth line was opened
eighteen seventy, crossing Cronkeyshaw; it's been
a footpath and a bridleway, but plans
have been proposed to make a Council tip.

Another group amongst the Irish folk
maintained itinerant traditions - twelve
described themselves as 'Travellers' and twenty
two as 'Hawkers'; there were 'Cutlers' too.
The summer months would find some labouring
on farms for haymaking and harvesting,
and very few in fact were unemployed.

Well ... Falinge Flats have covered some of it,
but Howard Street's still there and bits are left ...
of Wilson Street, and Hope Street Chapel built
in eighteen ten - and there on Redcross Street
the 'Abbey Inn' symbolically still marks
the place where 'potheen' flowed and Irish pipes
were played at funeral wakes. But nothing's left
to show why at beginning of this century
the policemen walked those streets in threes!

Jock McAvoy

On fourteenth January nineteen thirty
five, the landlord of the 'Abbey Inn'
brought in a wireless and positioned a
loudspeaker on the window ledge, so that
the regulars and passers-by could hear
the commentary on a boxing match.

'Jock McAvoy', 'The Rochdale Thunderbolt',
a local lad well-known around those streets,
was challenging the Frenchman, Marcel Thil,
for title of the European light-heavy
weight: he lost that fight, but was the British
Champion at middle weight from nineteen
thirty three to nineteen forty four,
and won the precious Lonsdale Belt outright.

He fought with stiffened thumb joints broken in
the cotton mill; his neck was broken in
a riding accident, but nothing stopped
him until polio when he was thirty
nine - and still his fists could pack a punch!
His real name was Joe Bamford; and his fighting
spirit died in nineteen seventy one.

Left: The route of the former Rochdale-Whitworth Railway line between Cronkeyshaw and Whitworth Road.

Photo: Copyright Rochdale Observer.

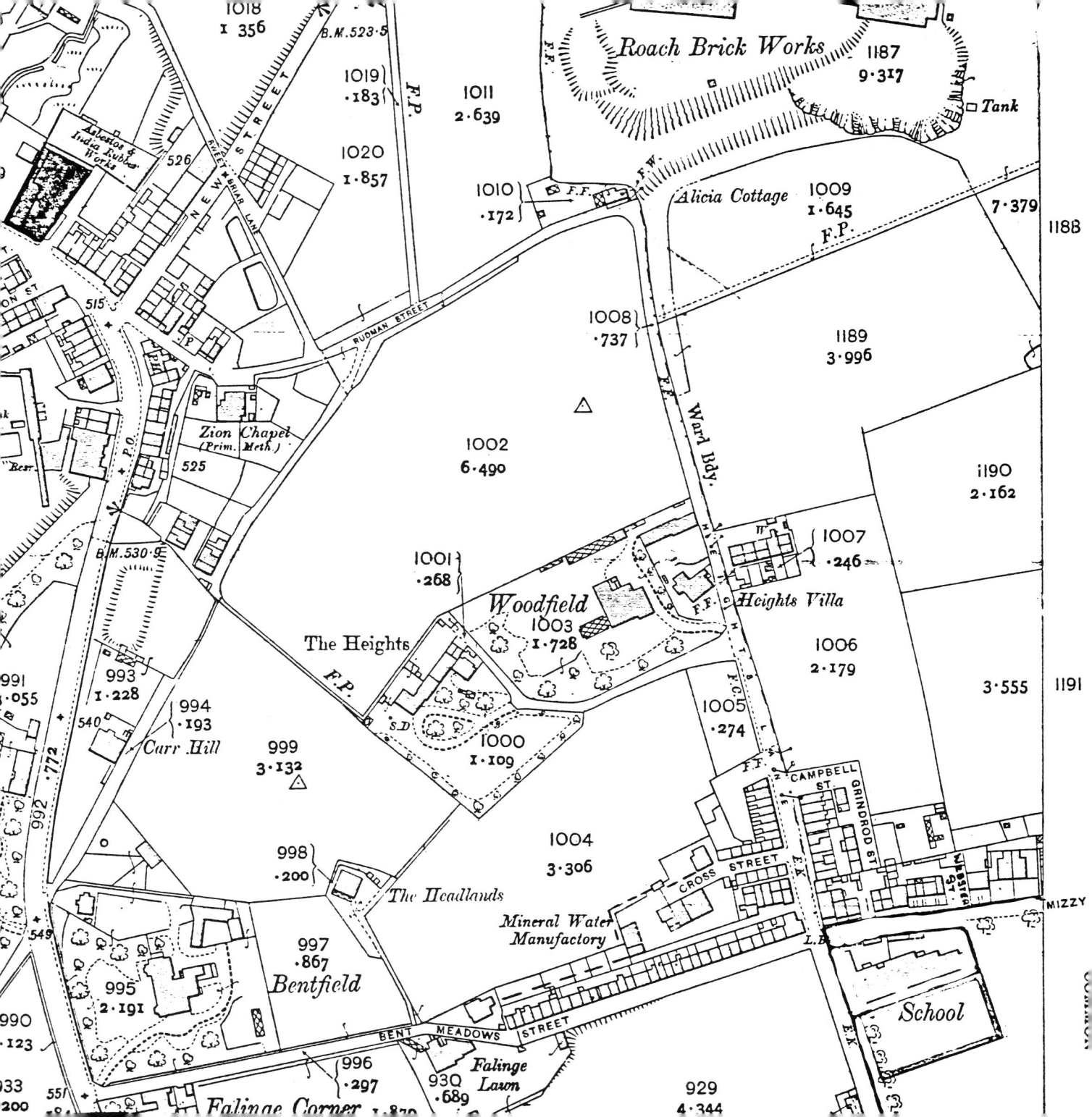

… TO 'THE HEIGHTS'

A view of Heights Lane 1988 from Falinge Flats. It shows what was once the top of Toad Lane until the 1850s. 'Quarry Hill' is just visible through the trees on the right, with the light gable end of 'Knowsley Villa' opposite, and Cronkeyshaw School at the top.

Left: The Ordnance Survey Map shows Heights Lane from Cronkeyshaw School to the top as it was in 1890.

Let's move back to the top of Heights Lane now. The map from eighteen ninety shows how it looked then; two centuries before, this was 'The Heights' Estate. A wall collapsed and killed a man whilst working on its post-war demolition (nineteen forties). So, where once 'The Heights' had space, the convolutions of Heights Avenue now dominate, but in the middle seventeen hundreds one John Clegg resided at 'The Heights' and farmed the land, with mineral workings in some parts as well.

Across Heights Lane a farm called 'Further Heights' was built in seventeen thirty seven. Frank Brierley, Heights Lane senior citizen, recalls his boyhood days round nineteen ten of haymaking at 'Further Heights'. From all this land, there's just one field that's not been built upon.

Old Deeds relating to 'Heights Villa', now re-named 'Heights End', reveal that Thomas Holme of 'Brown Hill' held the leasehold rights to what was then a field called Nearer Heights (a part of East Heights Field). He let it to be built upon in seventeen eighty two, as shown by the small inner section on the plan; but Whittakers were bound to give Holme access to collect all ashes and manure, and this strange option still holds good today!

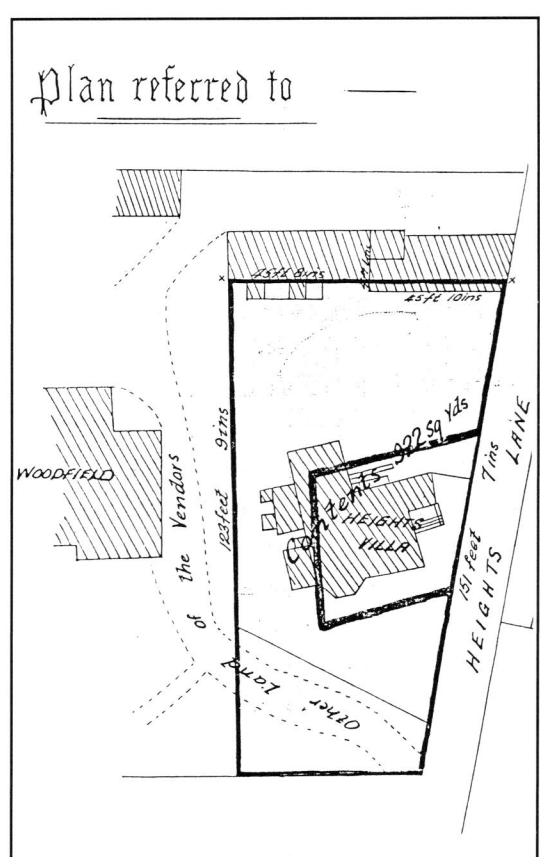

The dark outline of the inner section indicates the property built c.1782 which was used by the 'Guardians of the Poor' in 1847. The plan also shows the former drive leading to 'Woodfield'. See text pp80-84.

'From all this land, there's just one field ...'

The view down Heights Lane from near the top. On the left, Holt's Terrace (see text p84) down to Cronkeyshaw School; on the right, 'Heights End' down to 'The Bush' at the end of Bentmeadows. (See text pp92-95).

But by the year eighteen-o-two the much
more famous Taylors - Whitworth bonesetters
and doctors, whose manipulative skills
and herbal remedies were equally
applied to man and animal - owned part
of Heights Estate; and certainly from eighteen
twenty owned it all, because the Wills
of John and several Jameses vested it
in Betsy. Being a woman she could not
own property outright - her husband's name,
John Chadwick, is the one seen in the
Spotland Rates Book in connection with 'The Heights'
in eighteen thirty four. Her legal interests
in the land were managed by James Taylor
of Todmorden Hall, a doctor too
and 'Guardian of the Poor', whose home was ransacked
by a mob in eighteen thirty eight
in protest at enforcement of the Act
which separated husbands from their wives
and families in different Workhouses.

This was a reckless riot of despair.
The Todmorden and Rochdale 'Guardians'
successfully resisted the iniquitous
amendments to the Poor Laws as
John Cole's *'Down Poorhouse Lane'* reveals and
'Spotland Workhouse Diary' shows a more benign
than punitive approach to poverty.
Thomas Livsey's leadership from eighteen
forty on secured a respite which
the poor elsewhere in England were denied.

The building on the site 'Heights End' now stands
was let for seven years in eighteen forty
seven. Who to? Those 'Guardians of the Poor'
who used it as a 'fever ward' for such
poor wretches of the Workhouse as fell victim
to tuberculosis, typhus and
diphtheria, with little hope of cure.

Extracts from the Spotland Workhouse Weekly Diary 1836-1845 (Manuscript) written in the days when the Spotland Select Vestry was responsible. When the Union of Guardians finally took over in 1845, the need for a sanatorium or 'fever ward' was recognised, and the property on Heights Lane rented 1847-54. For the location of Spotland Workhouse at the end of what is now Primrose Street, off Spotland Road, see map p.4.

Written by the master, Alexander Cheetham

1838. Oct 31st Edmd Meadowcroft Died yesterday aged 74 years oure Fameley for a good while has been 70 and upwards and now we cannot number 50

Novr 7th we have nothing pertacular to relate this Week

14th Novr we had a Woman Hannah Brownhill came here this Day Week she began to be Poorley soon after she came and Died this Morning

5th Decr we have in the House to Day 29 Men 20 Women 2 Boys and 4 Girls we had an Irishman brought here in a Gigg yesterday that has been hurt on the Railway

Written by the master, Abraham Leach

On the 18th of August (1843) a woman of the name of Betty Clegg came into the House very poorly. The Doctor says she has a Cancer in the womb. The smell that she causes is very disagreeable. The Doctor said I must tell you that there aught to be a room on purpose for such as are afflicted with nauceous & infectious disorders, so that Fevers ... may be prevented from becoming epedimical among the inmates.

Feby 21rst (1844)
Our number is now 94. Since last report two have died, and four have come in. On Saturday John Pickup died of Consumption aged 77 years ...

We have had the Fever in the House for these four, or five weeks past. It was first brought in by a young man of the name of John Tattersall, and the Wednesday after John Mills wife came in. She had been waiting in a family in Manchester, who were all down of Typhus Fever; and the Saturday after she came in she took her bed. James Harrison and old James Fletcher, the Tailor, both have it at present.

Charles Walker, manufacturer of skips,
insurance agent of St. Mary's Gate,
erected new 'Heights Villa' and with Ann,
his wife, and children - five in all - he lived
in modest style, with just one servant/cook,
Jane Minnock, Scottish lass, the Census shows.
His mortgage with the Rochdale Borough Benefit
had Thomas Livsey, Chartist, as Trustee.
Three sixty pounds sounds now a modest sum!

And written in the Deeds is the condition
that the house must not be used again
as any kind of sanatorium;
and certain other occupations of
a 'noxious' character were subject to
consent, like beerseller, or blacksmith, pipe
or boiler maker, working brazier,
or slaughterman, or anyone who boiled glue
or size or soap, or tallow chandler ...

So Linda Thorpe's intention to hold
residential courses in the fragrant art
of floristry would surely be approved!
Not just for teaching floral decorative
techniques, from dainty bridesmaids' headdresses
to challenging displays on restaurant
ceilings - how to run a florist's business too.

The present building dates from eighteen fifty
four when more land was acquired; the
'fever ward' was levelled to the ground - but still
the cellars of 'Heights End' hold secrets of
those earlier times when clothes were scrubbed on slop
stones and the water pumped by servant hands.

Front view of 'Heights End' built as 'Heights Villa' c.1854.

Photo: Len Shaw

> We whose names are hereunder written being the within named Trustees of the Rochdale Borough Benefit Building Society do hereby declare that the within named Charles Walker has paid to us all Monies intended to be secured by the within written Indenture and payable to us in pursuance thereof and according to the Rules and regulations mentioned or referred to in the same Indenture – As Witness our hands this twenty third day of March One thousand and eight hundred and sixty three –
>
> Witnessed to all the signatures
> Jno Josh Moore
> Clerk to Holgate Swt &
> Roberts
> Solrs
> Rochdale
>
> Charles Walker
> Thomas Livsey
> George Maxwell
> Oliver Ormerod

Extract from the document showing Charles Walker had paid off his mortgage of £360 in nine years.

Rochdalians involved in local
politics this century will recollect
the Normantons and the Kay-Menzies both
resided at 'Heights End' at different times.

Which leaves the one remaining mystery
of why the gateposts to 'Heights Villa' or
'Heights End' are those belonging to 'Wood Field' -
the chiselled name is weathered in the stone.

By eighteen fifty nine John Chadwick was
deceased and Betsy left 'The Heights' to live
at Wath-on-Dearne. The rest of East Heights Field
was leased to Frederick Brown from South America,
a merchant of some kind. He built
'Wood Field', whose driveway cut across the foot
of what was Walker's plot before. (See plan)

The house was larger than 'Heights Villa' - it
had space for seven members of Brown's
family and three to cook and nurse and clean;
and then within ten years it housed thirteen.
But didn't stand the test of time so well,
so Woodfield Avenue now occupies
its space and only gateposts tell the tale.

The field below East Heights was Cross Field, hence
Cross Street; and opposite, Holt's Terrace (on
the eighteen nineties map as well) - farm
cottages of 'Further Heights' perhaps - could well
have been erected by John Holt of
Stubby Lee, who was involved with Heights Estate
as one Executor of James Taylor's Will,
and relative by marriage as the chart
of Taylors' genealogy reveals ...
though this idea has not been verified.
John Holt was also 'Guardian of the Poor' for
Wardleworth and Spotland Workhouses.

Behind the 'folksy' image of the Taylors
as the farriers and 'vets', who then
attracted rich and poor from far and wide
and treated all 'first come, first served', they did
accumulate enormous wealth and this
could not have been from charging eighteen pence
a week or from their presents from the rich.
It's thought they could have been of yeoman stock ...
but read West's book to get a full account.

James Taylor of Todmorden Hall d.1872

'The Whitworth Doctors'
Extract from Genealogical Chart of the Taylors

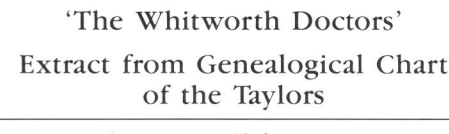

```
                                    James Taylor
                                      'Farrier'
                                       d.1752
                                          |
     ┌────────────────┬──────────┬────────┬───────┬─────────────────┐
*James Taylor = Betty     Henry   George  Sarah   *Edmund Taylor = Mary
 of Whitworth  of Extwistle                        of Heywood     d.1782
 d.1777        d.1789                              d.1784
     |                                                 |
  ┌──┴────────────┐                              ┌─────┴──────────┐
*‡John Taylor = Mary    *George Taylor = Betty   *Edmund Taylor  *John Taylor
 of Whitworth  d.1804    of Whitworth   of Glossop of Heywood    of Heap
 d.1802                  d.1804         d.1830     d.1814       'Cow Doctor'
     |                        |                                  d.1778
 ┌───┴─────────┐          ┌───┴────────────┬──────────────────┐
*‡James Taylor *‡John Taylor = Alice  Elizabeth = ‡James Maden *James Joseph = Anne of      *George Taylor
 of Whitworth  of Lockwood   d.1827  Taylor    of Greens       Hague Taylor of  Scaithcliffe  of Whitworth
 d.1826        d.c.1803              d.1845    d.1849          Todmorden Hall  d.1848        d.1831
     |                                                         d.1810
 ┌───┴──────────┬────────────────┐          ┌───────────────────┴──────────────┬─────────┬─────────┐
*‡James Taylor = Jane   ‡Betsy = ‡John Chadwick  Betsy = *‡James Taylor of = Mary Ann *John    *George   *Joseph
 of Whitworth          Taylor   d.c.1858         d.1838  Todmorden Hall    d.1864    Taylor   Taylor    Crossley
 d.1848                b.1800                            d.1872                      d.1827   d.1829    Taylor
     |                                                                                                  d.1836
     |                              Judith Maden = ‡John Holt
     |                              d.1843         of Stubby Lee
     |                                   |
 ┌───┴───────┐                    ┌──────┴──────┐      ┌──────┬──────────┬──────┬─────────┬──────────┐
*James Eastwood = Lavinia        James M. Holt  Emily S. Holt James   Mary = Henry  Arnold  *Herbert   *Alexander
 Taylor         d.1915            b.1829        Novelist      Taylor  d.1876  Cecil          Coupland   d.1884
 of Whitworth                                    d.1874       d.1848                         Taylor
 d.1876                                                                                      d.1891
```

* Practised medicine
‡ Involved with 'The Heights' Estate

Based on the chart in 'The Taylors of Lancashire' by John L. West and amended in the light of research from the Deeds of 'Heights End'. The photograph of James Taylor is from the same source.

Weavers' Cottages
Corner Mizzy Road.

Old cottages in Headlands Street and Bamford
Place have been done up - more fortunate
than weavers' cottages across the road,
with staircases of solid stone within,
that members of the 'Civic' tried to save.

The house 'The Headlands' (also on the map
of eighteen ninety), thought to have been built
around the eighteen twenties, is quite odd.
The Deeds confirm it was at one point owned
by Clement's grandson, Edmund Albert
Nuttall Royds, third son of Albert Hudson Royds.
A look at its construction would suggest
an economical approach - consistent
with a bailiff's house, head gardener,
or other manager of an Estate?
It lacks the trappings of the gentry of
the day, but, even when the well-known
Doctor Henry Brierley lived there, had a glass
conservatory all along the front.

It's now the home of Bob and Judith Brierley
(no relation), but whose family business,
Brierley's Springs, stood on Toad Lane for sixty
years across the road from 'Waljan' Mill.
The photo shows the way it started in
a former grocer's shop at fifty four
Toad Lane, when Edmund Brierley, bored in his
retirement, set up business once again.

'The Headlands', Bentmeadows in 1950.

The burnt-out roof of Brierley's Springs. 15th February 1976. This view from Waterhouse Street also shows 'Waljan' Mill on Toad Lane on the right.   Photo: Ashton

Brierley's Springs started here. This is the front view of the same stretch of Toad Lane c.1900. Howard's was No. 54.

Left: *Brierley's Springs in 1975.*
Photo: Reeves Maxwell

The Brierleys first became involved with springs in Shawclough Village: Edmund's father, James (in partnership with Kershaw) started what became four generations' lifetime's work. When Arthur Brierley, one of Edmund's sons, took on the business, really medicine was his first choice of career, but his son Bob began in nineteen forty nine by choice.

From nineteen nineteen on the business grew; extensions added nineteen thirty nine and sixty; cottages at front and rear demolished to make way ... but up until the fourteenth February nineteen seventy six, the office block was still 'Old Howard's Grocer's Shop'. That night an arsonist caused damage of a hundred thousand pounds.

It is no longer Brierleys' firm - bought out by Robert Riley in the nineteen sixties; there've been other takeovers since then. The building now has Williams (Painters) in.

'The Headlands' serves as a reminder of
the hierarchy of servants who performed
their duties in the service of the
'better off', from housemaid in St. Mary's
Vicarage to bailiff of the Royds' Estate.

They came from mainly rural districts
nationwide, and very few were Rochdale born.
The coachmen, gardeners, grooms and butlers had
more chance of permanent employment with
one master, whilst a governess or nurse
or house-cum-laundry maid might stay as long
as growing families dictated need.
The old retainers were remembered in
the master's Will: Jon. Fildes bequeathed the sum
of ten shillings per week for life to James,
his faithful servant, and five hundred pounds
to Martha and to Ruth in a lump sum.

When Clement Molyneux Royds lived at 'Green Hill'
in eighteen eighty one, seven servants kept
the household running smoothly: Minnie Windsor
was the housekeeper from Middlesex,
and no doubt Mary Freeston, underhousemaid,
kept the dust from worrying the stuffed
dogs in the hall - one had a small bag round
its neck because it used to fetch the post.

Clement Molyneux Royds

The duty of a bailiff twice a year
was to collect all ground rents on the many
properties comprising Royds' Estate.
Inside the marquees set up on the grass
of Lenny Barn were trestle tables laid
with cold roast beef and pickles - cook was
Betsy Anderson from Merionethshire.
This practice carried on into this
century: the grandmother of Judith Brierley
put her bonnet on and drove the dogcart,
with just room for one child by her side.
The rent was paid ... and then they stayed for lunch!

The old house was demolished and the present
building dates from nineteen thirty five.
'Green Hill' became the Grammar School for Girls,
and then a secondary school, and now
amalgamation makes it 'Falinge Park'.
The time-worn links with Royds are present yet.

Albert Hudson Royds, an invalid in his later years, in the grounds of 'Green Hill', built 1764.

Well, having strayed across the other side
of Falinge Road, return now to the map.
James Taylor owned the cottages erected
in Bent Meadows - eighteen twenty three.
That part was known as James Street for a while.
Though nearer to the bar the older ones
are thought to have been built for workers in
the mines which ran beneath Heights Lane (and
are referred to in the Deeds relating to
'Heights End'). Was this the Fishwicks' enterprise?

The occupants were mostly weavers still
in eighteen forty one, but evidence
of other trades remains: at number twenty
has been found a previous owner's keepsake
of his trade: an old glass bottle, green
and oddly shaped, belonged to G.T. Chadwick,
soda water manufacturer.
He lived there eighteen eighty one - the bottling
factory was just behind the row.

The cottage at the end was once 'The Bush',
the weavers' inn - it's good the name's been kept.
And since it's gone 'The Rifleman's' done well!
In nineteen fifty six this likelihood
was forecast by a pencilled note in Manor
Brewery's ledger … "Nearest house, 'Bush Inn',
to go eventually …" The 'Rifleman's'
was there in eighteen forty seven - it could
well date from eighteenth century times, and owned
by Royds till eighteen sixty when they sold
the leasehold, still retaining chief rent dues.

No written clue remains to tell us how
it got its name, but Royds had military
connections at the time; and soldiers who
were billeted in Barrack Yard at bottom
of Toad Lane marched up Parade Street to
the common land of Cronkeyshaw to drill.

RIFLEMANS ARMS
AND STONE COTTAGES
DATED 1720

These barracks opened eighteen thirty one
and closed in eighteen forty six. It seems
that Regiments of Highlanders were there,
and those who went to Sunday chapel joined
Blackwater Unitarians, whose service
suited Scottish Presbyterians.

The Sergeants frequented 'The Rose', an old
inn on Toad Lane, and lower ranks had ale
slipped out to them through 'The Hole i'th' Wall'.
A punishment parade was held for soldiers
who'd deserted and were caught, and they
were 'branded' with a 'D' in their disgrace!

But let's not leave 'The Bush' so easily, because it used to be the centre of this little Cronkeyshaw community. Directly on this Rochdale-Burnley Road, it's said it was the half-way post for stage coaches from Newhey through to Bacup. Travellers straight from Syke to Spotland passed 'The Rifleman's' and then 'The Bush' before proceeding down Bent Meadows, Falinge Fold, and downhill to the Spod and Rooley Moor.

The artist's impression of how 'The Bush' once looked. The wording on the gable end is 'as remembered'. By 1941 it had become a Cornbrook Brewery house.

The wanderings of Ben, the besom-maker,
and his donkey, Dimple, made immortal
by the pen of Edwin Waugh, would take
these paths as he delivered brooms to
'Talbot's Head', Shawclough, the Royds and Jacob Bright.
Preparing for his daily rounds, Ben told
his good wife Betty: "I've six for th'
Tobe's Yed; an' six for Clement's at th' Failinge;
and six for Owd Jacob's at Cronkyshay."
To follow Ben will take you up beyond
Shawclough to Chadwick's Healey Hall ... to Whitworth
Doctors' practice ... on to Lobden Moor.

View of Shawclough Road leading to Whitworth, from the back of 'The Talbot's Head', Rudman Street (see Map p76).
Photo: C. Lewis

Edwin Waugh's Besom Ben and Dimple

In nineteen twenty four 'The Bush' and
'Talbot's Head' were put under surveillance by
a plain-clothes policeman posing as a stranger
to the town, because a bookmaker
was taking bets illegally. The pub
fraternity soon 'sussed him out', so he
was forced to take an extra job at Turner's
to maintain his credibility.

From nineteen forty one to when it closed
on New Year's Eve in nineteen fifty six,
the Ashworth family had run 'The Bush'.
Their daughter Irene married from the inn
and still lives on Heights Lane - her sister,
Cissie Ashworth, was its final landlady.
She talks about companionship and
wartime outings; and the neighbours bringing jugs
and bowls for water when supply was off.
Beneath the cellars of 'The Bush' there is
a well - the pump's there yet - so there was
frequently a surplus keeping barrels cool!

In spite of fervent protest and petition
(ninety seven signatures in all)
this well-loved local had to close, as
structurally unsuitable and surplus to
the area's needs, and other reasons given.

So, yes, it's good the name's been kept - an old
inn sign which comes from Roman times when sale
of wine was advertised by signs which showed
a bush of evergreens, or were they vines?
But "Good wine needs no bush" - proverbially!

Whilst speculating on the origin of names, let's throw some light on Cronkeyshaw, which has been thought so similar to Cronkeyshinnagh in the Isle of Man as to support the view that 'cronk' is Celtic for 'a hill' and 'shinnagh' stands for 'foxes' ... and conveniently there's Foxholes near at hand.

But 'shaw' is not at all uncommon in these parts and can mean 'sheltered place' or sometimes 'little wood'; and nothing in old Deeds, or in its derivation, shows that it could possibly have links with 'shinnagh' ... so it's worth another look. To do this, first consider other names surrounding it.

The 'bench' or 'bent' in Bench Carr and Bent Meadows is the local name for 'coarse grass of the fens' and 'carr' itself means 'swamp'; that strange word 'mizzy' - 'moisture-laden dirt or mire'; and at the other end is Syke, 'a dried out water furrow' or 'a rivulet'.

It's clear that long before the ground dried out to be the ancient 'waste and common land' known variously as Crankshaw, Cronkashaye or Cronkayshawe, it was quite wet! So, for a fitting definition of the name of CRONKSHAW, look to Ekwall's book to find Old English 'cranuc/cronuc' meaning CRANE - a long-legged water-wading bird which came to SHELTER until migratory flight.

Now Fishwick recommended extreme caution in proposing Celtic origin as having bearing on this name ... so is it now more plausible to think of Cronkeyshaw as once a sanctuary for cranes?

Geoff Wood

Photo: Cyril Taylor, Ampthill

The cottages next door to 'Rifleman's'
on Mizzy Road were also owned by Royds,
built seventeen twenty as the date stone shows.
The first of these sold balm herb salve as well -
remembered by an old man passing by,
whose mother bought the healing ointment there.

And in another live an artist and
his wife, Geoff Wood and Edith, who've been 'Heights
Lane residents' since nineteen thirty eight.
He had associations with the Rochdale
School of Art, as student first, then teacher
in the pre-war years, then joined the 'RAF',
and Edith worked for 'Libraries and Arts'.

Primarily an artist always, but
his talents came in useful in designs
for signs and shops, and non-commercial things -
like making banners for a number of
the churches in the town ... St. Edmund's Church,
whose Scouts the Woods both helped to organise.

St. Edmund's Church Whit Walk passing Blackwater Street Unitarian Chapel (early 1960s). In the background, St Mary's Parsonage, and 'The Rising Sun' on Cheetham Street.

Edith Wood

A very unassuming man, Geoff Wood's
a member of the British Artists'
Federation and has work shown at the 'Mall'
and other Galleries, and also at
the 'Royal Academy' ... but still enjoys
the weekly Rochdale Artists' get-together
at 'Greenhill', though in his seventies now.

A genuine rusticity pervades
their home ... rough wooden beams, unplastered
stonework framing gentle watercolour scenes
that caught the artist's eye in England and
abroad - the wider world inside a room.

And Rochdale memories to fill a book,
but simple images stay close to mind ...

The Lord Street lamp and letterbox combined
that stands outside Toad Lane Museum now.
The market bargains late on Saturdays
when fruit and fish all had to go because
they had no fridges in those pre-war days.
A girder left 'suspended' all throughout
the War when work on market building stopped.
John Buyright's way of selling "Cigarettes,
a box of chocolates and something else
for half a crown!" The smell of firelighters
and paraffin in Starlight Mantle shop.
The bar that closed Exchange Street once a year.
And big stone bee-hive off a Toad Lane Co-op
shop that's now in new St. Mary's Place.

The artist's recollection of the bottom of Toad Lane ... on the left hand side

The outdoor market and the bar that closed Exchange Street once a year — about 1930.

... and on the right

George Keelty is another gentleman who's witnessed all this century's changes in Toad Lane. His family had a Brewery on Heights Lane, and other interests in property built on the land the Fildes once owned.

Born nineteen ten and christened at St. Mary's Church, he grew up at the 'Rising Sun' on Cheetham Street and went to school at first in Redcross Street, the National School by name.

When he was in his early teens he used to go to 'pictures' every Tuesday at the Empire (opposite Town Hall) to watch 'The Hooded Terror' serial with Pearl White, and then ran up Toad Lane for fish and chips at Haigh's, with dandelion and burdock too. He savoured this from one week to the next!

And when the Brickcroft Club went up in flames, the kids dashed down to watch, and he was there.

He taught in several Rochdale schools and organised schools' sports for many years; in fact, Pete Coleman, landlord of the 'Brownhill' pub, was one of many local lads he taught.

George Keelty 1988
In the background, the facade of 'Mount Falinge' in Falinge Park.

He talks of Co-op's Reading Room, with Marcroft's Toffee Shop next door, the sportswear shop - Brookes' Stores, and all the other shops that Toad Lane had ... George Glazzard's Brushworks, which supplied the means to clear the streets of Rochdale in the winter when it snowed ... and then the Saw Mills round by Hudson Street where Falinge Flats cut through ... And now in his retirement he looks out on Falinge Park where on the hill the ruins of Royds' mansion stand; and on fine days the view is brightened by the splash of Asian silks and satins on green lawns.

The Rochdale Emblem incorporating the weighing of the fleece, woolsack, weight stones, cotton buds and martlets.

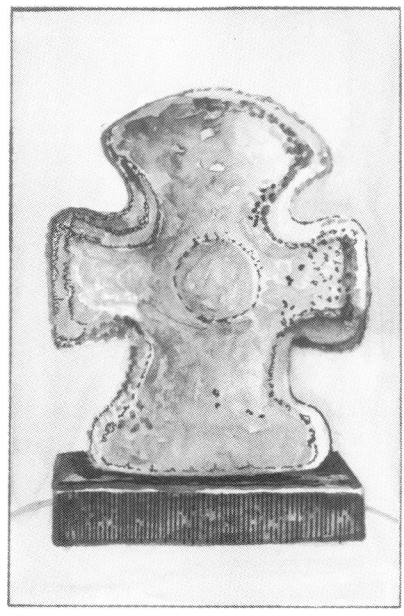

The Market Cross

Rochdale Market's multi-racial now –
a place to see the population-mix
in microcosm ... Permission for the town
to hold a market was first granted in
eleven ninety eight, it's said; though later
on, when Henry Third was King, he gave
the town a Charter. People who made goods
and woven cloth took these to market to
be sold; unfinished cloth was sold for export
or despatched to local fulling mills.

The market had a growing reputation
around fifteen sixty eight when Bury's
Rector chose to leave a gift by Will
(to feed one hundred of his Parish poor)
of "half a hope of ote mele" or the cash
to buy it with, as priced "in Rachedale Marketh".

The market's been for many centuries
on sites around the bottom of Toad Lane.
The old stone Market Cross where haltered wives
were brought like cattle to be sold, perhaps
for two 'bob' each, was taken down in
seventeen eighty five. The sculptured sheep in
Yorkshire Street now mark the entrance to the
present market via the shopping 'Mall'.

The bulldozers on the site of the bottom market 1973

... and how it used to be

The old market hall

Outdoor and indoor markets of the past

The eighteenth century flannel market was on Mondays in Blackwater Street. And in November eighteen thirty eight, firearms were sold all cheaply priced when Chartist sympathisers were campaigning for their rights.

The Brierley family had a say in its affairs as well when Joseph Brierley, J.P. was the Market Company's Chairman in eighteen seventy four. The Company first built a market hall in eighteen twenty three. Before that time the stalls had cluttered Yorkshire Street (a mere fifteen feet wide) and nothing could get through ... but now of course the Market Company is no more, and Rochdale Council holds a long-term lease from Laings and C.I.S. (Co-op Insurance) too.

Left: About 1895 — The bottom market and the 'Clock Face', 'Coach and Horses' and 'Griffin' inns.
(Photos: from D. Freedman's collection)

The market's seen some changes in the last
one hundred years and there are market
families that span that time and even more.

The oldest are the Halliwells who sell
the flowers and plants from their own nursery.
Five generations now have worked a market
stall: first grandfather to Madge stood by
the pig market last century, then father
Tom on Yorkshire Street; now Madge, her son
and granddaughter - the present and the future.

Next oldest are the Haywards, selling fish,
who always stood 'outside' till nineteen seventy
five - and they go back a hundred years.

Then Jordans, meat and poultry, and the
Beresfords in household textiles, started
after First World War; and Kayes with millinery,
and Bentleys with greengrocery, from nineteen
thirty eight ... And some of them recall
the inside market burning down when they
were young in nineteen thirty seven; some traders
lost 'the lot' - not much insurance then.
But folk were glad when rats that ran up Yorkshire
Street in packs all vanished in the fire!

This happened not long after Market Company
had sold out to Rochdale Corporation
who, mindful of the special time of year,
then took on ninety joiners all at once
to make a wooden floor across old Baths
in Smith Street; stalls were built and signs were made,
so market didn't lose its Christmas trade.

The market was rebuilt with meat and fish
all facing South to 'ripen' in the sun!
But never finished when the War broke out.

Old market families ... in the 1988 setting

Kaye's millinery

Haywards' fish stall

The oldest lady of the oldest market family: Madge Glazzard of Halliwell's ...

... and son Mark.

New market faces ...

Margaret Campbell (left) started selling hats on the outside market in February 1988. She is chatting to Denise Barnes who used to sell American Football gear.

M. Saleem (an electrical engineer) has had a market stall since 1984.

Fashion garments sold on the market illustrate part of the Asian community's contribution to the commerce of the town.

Somewhere to pass the time of day ...

Derek May of Bentley & May. The firm has sold greengrocery on Rochdale Market since 1938.

And now the market's moved from this old site.
Most of these traders and the management
agree, compared with where the market used
to be, the present situation's not
so good for passing trade. They hope for something
better in due course. Their trade's been hit
as well, they say, by popularity
of supermarkets nowadays. It's also
felt it lacks the atmosphere the nineteen
sixties' market had ... and traders talk
with fondness of their snacks at Marshall's 'Caf',
and taking jugs for soup with dumplings in,
and hot U.C.P. tripe ... a jar at lunchtime
in 'Clock Face' or Toad Lane's 'Market House' -
a dingy place, but good to socialise
around the open fire ... It's not the same!

Yet ... Derek May still shouts the price of cauli's
out like market traders always did!

There's folk in Rochdale still who miss the bottom
market on Toad Lane, where stalls hung flaring
lamps of kerosene, though it's been gone
since nineteen seventy three - October twenty
seventh to be precise, and Toad Lane
demolition started three weeks after that.
It was a time of great uncertainty
when threat of loss of work made traders
lobby councillors to find another site.
They moved to Hunters Lane and Cheetham Street.

Of Rochdale Market's characters, one man, Dougie Freedman, is renowned; for many years he captivated customers by auctioning his goods with geniality.

He was the spokesman for the traders when the fight was on to keep the market where it was and do it up, but Laings, the property developers, had other plans which minimised the many access points the former market had and pushed it to the back of Rochdale's Shopping Precinct.

He left ... and has a busy little 'indoor market' of his own on Baillie Street - and plans to write the story of his life. But if he mentions somewhere how he once displayed his wares on ground quite near the precincts of St. Mary's Church, he'll no doubt fail to mention that he later made a generous contribution to the restoration fund ... but that's the sort of man he is.

Douglas Freedman in his market days.

The story of the graveyard in The Baum
cannot explain why phantoms have been seen,
but is of special interest nonetheless.

The present church is wider than the old,
and in the course of building it some burial
places were disturbed and coffins lifted
from the ground to be interred elsewhere -
all well-preserved by virtue of the stream's
effects. The names of tiny children could
be read on silver plates still shining bright ...
and so it was, much later, when the great
upheaval of the seventies took place.

This happened after twenty years of talk
amongst officials of the town, on rights
and wrongs of deconsecrating ground to
make a road to ease the traffic problem.

But it was done in nineteen seventy four.
The lead-lined oaken caskets were removed;
and Hunters Lane cut straight across The Baum,
with Woolworths building partly on the spot
where Rochdale's long deceased had lain in
hallowed ground ... So progress makes its mark! And as
with Rochdale's industries, the ebb and flow
of growth, decline and need to modernise
is felt within the churches in its midst.

St. Mary's Church combines traditional
services (as in the Prayer Book sixteen
sixty two) with warmth and informality
in all parochial relationships.
And once again the building's had to be
substantially repaired, but times have changed.
No more are wealthy individuals
connected with the church: the Chethams and
the Brierleys and the Cromptons have all gone.

So now it seems it's up to Conservation
Trusts like English Heritage, but still
to individuals in smaller ways
to keep such buildings for posterity.

Reverend Melville Hall, Vicar of St. Mary's, retired Easter 1988. He organised the most recent restoration work.

Goodbye to old Toad Lane

We've wandered up and down and round about
from Toad Lane to 'The Heights'. We never can
know everything ... just learn a little more.
So, back to where we started. Final thoughts!

The church has lost its graveyard and The Baum
has lost its herb ... but saddest thing of all
would seem to be that having spanned so many
centuries, and two World Wars in tact ...
NOW Toad Lane's real identity has been
obscured by bulldozers' indifference.

It's true the Conservation Area
reflects the past - the weavers, shopkeepers
and publicans - yet sad, in view of its
historical significance, it's lost
vitality and continuity.

What must have started as a pathway from
the river bank has had its lifeline cut.
But this once busy Rochdale tollgate route
- *yes, ever. in its shabby sixties' days* -
had unique character ... epitomised
by landlords of the likes of Billy Luff
and Allan Ellis - up to twenty years
of service in their woollen merchants' inns,
'The Coach and Horses' and 'The Old Clock Face'.

Toad Lane in the 'shabby sixties'

The Fox and Dog ... to St. Mary's Vicarage

'The Old Clock Face' and 'Coach and Horses'
Photos: A. Marshall

Frank Turner in the 1950s.

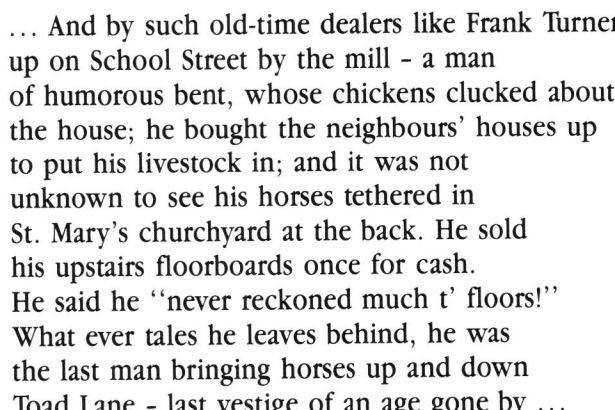

Frank Turner's cottages were on the right at the bottom of School Street, just behind Brierley's Springs.

'The little bit that's been conserved ...'

The Pioneers, Birkett's opticians and Morris's. Beyond, the Central Pioneers, with stone beehive on top.

... And by such old-time dealers like Frank Turner
up on School Street by the mill - a man
of humorous bent, whose chickens clucked about
the house; he bought the neighbours' houses up
to put his livestock in; and it was not
unknown to see his horses tethered in
St. Mary's churchyard at the back. He sold
his upstairs floorboards once for cash.
He said he "never reckoned much t' floors!"
What ever tales he leaves behind, he was
the last man bringing horses up and down
Toad Lane - last vestige of an age gone by ...

... But mainly by the shopkeepers with years
and years of trading in Toad Lane ... so here's
a final tribute to the Morrises,
who were 'The Co-op Shop's' close neighbours for
more than fifty years. Such special folk,
with so much more than just an old
ironmonger's shop, called 'Ratchda's Treasure Shop'
by poet Kenneth Hill, who captured well
the sense of loss when ordinary familiar
things must go, to make way for the new.

A shame Toad Lane will never be the same!

And so much more than just the little bit
that's been conserved that shouldn't be forgotten.

Marcia Bartlett
1987/1988

Rachda's Treasure Shop

Mrs. Catherine Morris

The Baum Restaurant now occupies these premises.

Photo: M.T. Bentley

Owd Morris's shop wor a treasure
An' full up wi' o' sorts o' things,
Like tay-pots, an' kettles, an' brushes,
An' curtain rods complete wi' rings.
A basket for one an' a tanner,
Or black-lead to do up yur grate;
A hinge or a rasp or a spanner,
A lock an' a bolt for yur gate.
A mantle or two for yur 'Tilly',
Some owd leather belt for yur shoon;
A last an' a hommer to mend wi',
A knife or a fork or a spoon.
A candle to put in yo' saucer;
A thingy to put under t' bed;
Some tongs for to mak' yur hair wavy,
An' curlers to put in yo' yed.
A tin mug an' plate fro' the Army,
A poker to push into t' coal;
An all maks o' different concoctions
To fill up all sizes o' hole.
Screwdrivers boath British an' Yankee,
Wire nettin' to do t' chicken run.
An' boxes an' tins full o' nick-nacks;
Aw've sorted through lots: it wor fun.

Owd bread crocks to keep all yo' bread in,
Flat-irons, an' some run on gas.
They'd possers an' owd fashioned mangles,
An' all maks o' things made o' brass.
Wash-leathers, an' dusters, an' graters,
'Pop' bottles to put in yo' bed;
A 'peeler' for 'Eyein' yo' taters,
Confetti for when yo' get wed.
A dolly-tub complete wi' washboard,
Egg-timers, some needles an' pins,
An' several mysterious objects
Put in 'unidentified' tins.
Yo' could get rubbin'-stones for yo' doorstep,
An' ladders boath step-ones an' long,
A birdcage; or dish for yo' doggy;
An' even a loud dinner gong.
There's lots o' more things Aw could mention,
O' t' shop near t' Co-op i' Toad Lane;
But now hoo's bin shifted to t' market
Aw doubt it'll ever be t' same.
Yo'll still get the same pleasant service
An' buy things they're makin' no more;
But Aw'll miss the *feelin'* inside me
When rootin' in Morris's store.

Ken Hill 1973

Sources of Reference

View of Toad Lane 1936 looking up to the junction with Falinge Road.

Unless otherwise stated books are in the Local Studies Section of Rochdale Reference Library.

1. Croston, 'History of Rochdale'.
2. Butterworth, 'Rochdale and Saddleworth' pub. 1828.
3. Oakley, G.R. (Vicar of St. Andrew's, Dearnley) 'In Olden Days' pub. 1923.
4. Kershaw, H. 'Growing Up'.
5. Kershaw, H. 'Over My Shoulder'.
6. Wadsworth, A.P. 'Rochdale's Main Roads: The History of Turnpikes' in Transactions of the Rochdale Literary and Scientific Society Vol XIII-XV.
7. Fishwick, H. 'The History of the Parish of Rochdale' pub. 1889.
8. Raines, Canon, 'The Vicars of Rochdale'.
9. Wild, A.S. 'Top o'th Steps' — A History of St. Chad's Parish Church, Rochdale.
10. Hill, K. Poem 'Ratchda's Treasure Shop' (Printed on reverse side of photograph of Morris's in Library's collection of Toad Lane; and in Hill, K. 'A little of what you fancy'.
11. Robertson, W. 'History of Rochdale Past and Present' pub. 1875.
12. Rochdale Observer, Series of articles 'Old Buildings Around Rochdale'.
13. Eyre, K. 'Lancashire Ghosts'.
14. Rochdale Observer (Supplement 1.10 .77.)
15. McKisack, 'The Fourteenth Century 1307-1399'. (Lending Library)
16. Wilkinson, B. 'The Later Middle Ages in England'. (Lending Library)
17. Cowie, L. 'The Black Death and Peasants' Revolt' (Documentary History Series). (Lending Library)
18. Nuttall, W. 'A Fragment: Intended as an introduction to the history of Rochdale' pub.1810.
19. Brierley, H. 'Reminiscences of Rochdale' pub. 1923.
20. Langford-Brown, A.R. (Vicar of St. Mary's Church) 'A short history of St. Mary's Parish, Rochdale'.
21. Taylor, 'Folk Speech of South Lancashire'.
22. Baron, 'A Lankisher Dickshonary'.
23. Rochdale and Heywood Express 30.10.87.
24. Wadsworth, A.P. 'The Myth of the Flemish Weavers' in Transactions of the Rochdale Literary and Scientific Society Vols. XXI-XXII 1941-46.
25. March, H.C. 'East Lancashire Nomenclature and Rochdale Names'.
26. Kershaw, H. 'Among my Souvenirs'.
27. Kershaw, H. 'Lancashire Mettle'.
28. Kershaw, H. 'The Day Before Yesterday'.
29. O.S. Maps 1851, 1877, 1890, c.1930
30. Allen, F. 'A brief history of education and schools in Rochdale'.
31. McGrath, W.J. 'Post Standard v. Educational Provision promoted by the Rochdale School Board 1870-1902'.
32. Cronkeyshaw School (Mixed Dept.) School Log Book 1893-1907.
33. Cronkeyshaw School (Infants School) School Log Book 1895-1900.
34. Advertisements outside Co-op Museum, Toad Lane.
35. Rochdale and Burnley Turnpike Road Minutes 1755-1791.
37. Information from Marie Kilgallon of W. & J. Sharples, Toad Lane.
38. Taylor, T.W. 'Points preserving the memory of places and buildings of local historic interest' in Transactions of the Rochdale Literary and Scientific Society Vols.XVII-XVIII 1929-34.
39. a) Census Records 1841; b) 1851; c) 1861 — Toad Lane/Heights Lane — Spotland/Wardleworth; d) 1871 and 1881 (as for c)
40. Rowe, W. (Canon) (Vicar of St. Mary's Church) 'Parish of St. Mary, Wardleworth, Rochdale' (from St. Mary's Church).
41. Information from Ormerods Ltd., Hanging Road, Rochdale.
42. Information from Rev. Melville Hall, Vicar of St. Mary's Church.
43. Information from Mr. Marcroft, Warden of St. Mary's Church.
44. Wadsworth, A.P. & de Lacy Mann, J. 'The Cotton Trade and Industrial Lancashire 1600-1780'.

45. Hopwood, E. 'A History of the Lancashire Cotton Industry and the Amalgamated Weavers' Association'.
46. Kay-Shuttleworth, Sir James, 'Public Education from 1846-1852'.
47. Nightingale, B. (Rev.) 'Lancashire Nonconformity'.
48. The Rochdale Nonconformist Vol. 2 No. 2 dated February 1898.
49. Robertson, W. 'The Life and Times of Right. Hon. John Bright'.
50. John Ashworth's Chapel for the Destitute Reports 1859-1922.
51. Census of Religious Worship 30th March 1851.
52. Rochdale Reform Association 150th Anniversary 1.12.84. (Envelope)
53. Popular Liberalism: Rochdale. Extracted from Vincent, J. 'The Formation of the Liberal Party 1857-68'.
54. Rochdale Town Development 1972-74 Press Cuttings — Rochdale Observer 10.3.72., 9.5.73., and 3.10.73.
55. Rochdale Town Centre District Plan Sept.1978 Final Proposals (Toad Lane Conservation Area).
56. Bright, J. 'The Diaries of John Bright' pub. 1930.
57. Rochdale's Alternative Paper, August 1973.
58. Heape, R. 'Inscribed and dated stones and sundials in and adjoining Rochdale'.
59. Information from Mr. Whitehead, Assistant Manager, Rochdale Market, and from the following market traders: Mrs. M. Glazzard (Halliwells), Mrs. Kaye, Mr. Hayward, Mr. Jordan, Mr. Beresford & Mr. D. May (Bentley & May).
60. (a) Information from Mr. D. Freedman, Baillie Street, Rochdale and (b) Mr. J. Cannon, Farrier, Heywood.
61. Information from Mr. G. Keelty, Sheriff Street, Rochdale.
62. Information from Mr. F. Brierley, Heights Lane, Rochdale.
63. Information from Mrs D. Greaves and publications, etc. in The Co-op Museum, Toad Lane, including Chart of Original Members compiled by Schill Laah Copes, J.F. and Crossley, G.
64. Cole, J. Dissertation 'Chartism in Rochdale' (a) Rochdale — the Social and Industrial Background (b) Chartism in Rochdale.
65. Robertson, W. 'Old and New Rochdale'.
66. Information from Mr. & Mrs. P. Coleman, The Brownhill Hotel, Heights Lane.
67. Information from Mr. Mills, A.H. Sutcliffe & Co., Yorkshire Street, Mr. G. Taylor, Taylor Engineering, Church Stile, and Mr. S. Ali, Wear Fine, School Street, Rochdale.
68. Robertson, W. 'A Social and Political History of Rochdale'.
69. Robertson, W. 'Rochdale and Vale of Whitworth'.
70. Fishwick, H. 'Rochdale in the beginning of the 17th century'.
71. Mattley, R.D. 'Annals of Rochdale'.
72. Royds, Sir C.M. 'Pedigree of Family of Royds'.
73. Lahee, 'Life of Thomas Livsey'.
74. Reeves, J. 'A Century of Rochdale Co-operation 1844-1944'.
75. Shercliff, W.H. '150 years on — A Short account of Peterloo'.
76. Bruton, F.A. 'The Story of Peterloo'.
77. Bamford, S. 'Portrait of a Radical'.
78. Robertson, W. 'Rochdale and the History of its Progress'.
79. Information from Mr. Frank Turner, Green Lane, Heywood.
80. Information from Mr. J. Rotherham, Bentmeadows, Rochdale.
81. (a) Information from Mr. R. Stables, Heights Avenue, Rochdale. (b) Article in Rochdale Observer by R. Stables 9.7.86.
82. Information from present owner, Alicia Cottage, Heights Lane, Rochdale.
83. Information from Mr. and Mrs. G. Wood, Mizzy Road, Rochdale.
84. Information from Mrs. L. Thorpe, 'Heights End', Heights Lane, Rochdale.
85. Information from resident in Holt's Terrace, Heights Lane, Rochdale.
86. Heape, C. & R. 'Records of the Family of Heape'.
87. Information from Samuel Smith's Brewery, Tadcaster.
88. Butt, John. (Ed.) 'Robert Owen — Prince of Cotton Spinners'.